ADVANCE PRAISE FOR *PASSION AT WORK*

"To find and pursue your passion is to be truly alive! *Passion at Work* is a wonderful tool to turn your passion into practice."

> —Cynthia Good, CEO and Founding Editor,
> *PINK* magazine

"It will surely motivate many people to take an aggressive approach in breaking the boundary between work and existence."

> —Nassim Nicholas Taleb, author of *Fooled by Randomness*, selected by *FORTUNE* to be included with all-time classics such as *The Wealth of Nations* and *The Art of War*

"Lawler Kang has written an impassioned work to help people find their own passion and satisfaction in their work. Equally important, drawing on his wide experience and insightful analysis, he also provides a practical and compelling roadmap on how to get there."

> —Daniel Yergin, author of the Pulitzer Prize-winning book, *The Prize* and *Commanding Heights*

"Kang gives us a lens into ourselves. By mastering the Five Ps—passion, proficiency, priorities, plan, and prove—we can take control of our lives and careers. The book offers timely and relevant ideas and tips. Based on Kang's remarkable personal experiences and will, he infuses the reader with a sense of purpose, meaning, and confidence."

> —Dr. David Ulrich, Professor at Ross School of Business, University of Michigan, co-author of *The HR Value Proposition*

"In today's 24/7 world, *Passion at Work* can help you find one thing that is far more important than money—meaning! An excellent book that combines making a living with making a difference."

> **—Dr. Marshall Goldsmith, globally acclaimed author and thought leader on leadership, named by *Forbes* as one of five most respected executive coaches**

"Kang's engaging book offers really useful ideas for how to live in a way that aligns your actions with your values. Doing so brings passion to your work and to the rest of your life. Read it now—and let the passion flow!"

> **—Dr. Stewart Friedman, Director of the Work/Life Integration Program, The Wharton School, named by *Working Mother* as one of the top 25 most influential people on work/family issues**

"This is a lively and interesting book on understanding and planning your work within the framework of your whole life. The concepts of the end game and understanding your passions, proficiencies, and priorities in putting together a business plan for yourself are well presented and make a lot of sense. An invaluable tool for anyone, wherever you are in your career."

> **—Michael Schoettle, Retired Partner, Heidrick & Struggles, world's premier executive placement firm**

"Passion—the 'magic bullet'—is at the core of achieving your potential. *Passion at Work* serves up a highly stimulating and compelling framework for self-reflecting and profiting—in every sense—by focusing on the one thing that matters most: staying true to your passion. Kang's own experiences and insights add keen perspective, while motivating any reader to act NOW."

> **—Robert Hargadon, General Manager, Corporate Learning Group, Microsoft**

PASSION AT WORK

PASSION AT WORK

HOW TO FIND WORK YOU LOVE AND LIVE THE TIME OF YOUR LIFE

Lawler Kang

Foreword by Mark Albion

An Imprint of Pearson Education

Upper Saddle River, NJ • New York • London • San Francisco • Toronto • Sydney •
Tokyo • Singapore • Hong Kong • Cape Town • Madrid •
Paris • Milan • Munich • Amsterdam

Library of Congress Cataloging-in-Publication Data

Kang, Lawler.
  Passion at work : how to find work you love and live in the time of your life / Lawler Kang,
Mark Albion.
    p. cm.
  ISBN 0-13-185428-3
  1. Vocational guidance—Psychological aspects. 2. Work—Psychological aspects
3. Job satisfaction. 4. Conduct of life. 5. Self-actualization (Psychology) I. Title: How to
find work you love and live in the time of your life. II. Albion, Mark S., 1951- III. Title.
  HF5381.K344 2006
  650.1—dc22

                                                                            2005016537

Vice President and Editor-in-Chief: *Tim Moore*
Acquisitions Editor: *Paula Sinnott*
Editorial Assistant: *Susie Abraham*
Development Editor: *Russ Hall*
Director of Marketing: *John Pierce*
International Marketing Manager: *Tim Galligan*
Cover Designer: *Chuti Prasertsith*
Managing Editor: *Gina Kanouse*
Senior Project Editor: *Lori Lyons*
Copy Editor: *Karen A. Gill*
Indexer: *Lisa Stumpf*
Compositor: *ContentWorks*
Manufacturing Buyer: *Dan Uhrig*

© 2006 by Pearson Education, Inc.
Publishing as Prentice Hall
Upper Saddle River, New Jersey 07458

Prentice Hall offers excellent discounts on this book when ordered in quantity for bulk
purchases or special sales. For more information, please contact U.S. Corporate and
Government Sales, 1-800-382-3419, corpsales@pearsontechgroup.com. For sales outside the
U.S., please contact International Sales, 1-317-581-3793, international@pearsontechgroup.com.

Company and product names mentioned herein are the trademarks or registered trademarks of
their respective owners.

Printed in the United States of America

Third Printing January 2006

ISBN: 0-13-185428-3

Pearson Education LTD.
Pearson Education Australia PTY, Limited.
Pearson Education Singapore, Pte. Ltd.
Pearson Education North Asia, Ltd.
Pearson Education Canada, Ltd.
Pearson Educatión de Mexico, S.A. de C.V.
Pearson Education—Japan
Pearson Education Malaysia, Pte. Ltd.

To Zan and Arion, boat rockers extraordinaire!

CONTENTS

ACKNOWLEDGMENTS

I'd like to thank everyone who has helped me understand what living is all about. This includes everyone with whom I've had the pleasure of studying, carousing, traveling, and working, particularly those from Scient. Chris Zikakis gets special note here for his personal contributions to the evolution of my thoughts, processes, and eventual genesis of this book. The staff and administration from my formal educations—Chadwick, Vassar, and Wharton—each of which contributed mightily to my appreciation of life (while putting up with me) also receive heartfelt thanks. In this context, various body parts of Jerry Martin and Debbie Merrill should be bronzed. Gerald Chertavian and the staff and students from Year Up also deserve recognition for their willingness to try out a struggling speaker and for their ongoing encouragement. Donna Modica, Marilyn Eckleman, Peter Degnan, Michelle Antonio, Chris Morris, Tom Monaco, and Ashley Chiampo also deserve their names in lights for their willingness to believe. I also want to spotlight Lisa Noble Kaneb for her observation/challenge that will forever stay with me.

Thanks to my behind-the-scenes support crew—Robert White, Lin Bumford, Roselyn Romberg, Jack Krawitz, Josh Klenoff, Allison Kluger, Bernie Conneely, Mick Perry and m360,

Bob Ezzell, Suzanne Lozzi, Tom Underwood, and Boris Savic and the Rocket North crew—for their assistance in bringing my platform to market. I'd also like to thank the lads from the Descendents, Soundgarden, Green Day, and XTC for their insane courage to literally rock the world and provide me my background music during this entire process. Extraordinary thanks to Russ Hall for his committed and impassioned developmental editing contributions and Paula Sinnott, my editor, who was willing to take a chance with this untested conglomeration of manic energy. Kudos to Waterside Productions and Craig Wiley, my agent, for their quick turnarounds. The next time I will expect a response in less than six hours!

Now, the real suspects. I have been exceptionally blessed to have acquired some exceptional traits from exceptional parents. Mom (and Joe), Dad (and Di), I will never be able to thank you enough for your genes (and their expressions), support, and belief in me. The same goes to Alex and Linda, newer on the scene, but whose contributions have indelibly left their mark. Finally, I would be nowhere right now if it weren't for my irascible sidekicking sister and my extraordinary wife. Thank you both, from the bottommost chasms of my soul, for simply being there.

I love you all!

April, 2005

ABOUT THE AUTHORS

Born and raised in suburban Los Angeles, **Lawler Kang** presently releases his passions in Manchester-by-the-Sea on Boston's North Shore. He is married, has two hooligans, and serves on numerous advisory boards. He relishes his time traveling, serving as a human jungle gym, skiing, skateboarding, and body-boarding, and lusts for time to play bridge. Additionally, drawing on the combined skills, values and experiences of his Passion Posse, he also recently founded LK Ventures LLC, a services firm geared to facilitate individual and corporate identification and alignment of passion.

Mark Albion, who wrote the Foreword for *Passion at Work*, is the author of the New York Times bestseller, *Making a Life, Making a Living*. Mark graduated from Harvard University and Harvard Business School, and taught at the latter. Mark is a successful entrepreneur and is a leader in bringing passion and faith to work.

FOREWORD

"What I do best is share my enthusiasm."

—Bill Gates

The most important source of competitive advantage in the twenty-first century will come from individuals and organizations that unleash the power of passion.

Many summers ago, I conducted a research project on retail profitability with a well-known investment-banking firm. Our task was to uncover five indicators that could predict which retailers would have the largest growth in stock valuation over the next five years. The second most important factor was something we "felt" in the home offices of the most financially successful firms. At the time, we described it as "a buzz, an air of excitement, of people working together to do something important." In a word, we were describing an enthusiasm that resulted from individual and team passion—a passion rooted in each person's personal connection with the company's missions and objectives and with each other.

Nearly two decades later—March 15, 2005, to be exact—I had lunch outdoors in the warm sunshine of Cape Town, South Africa with Colin Hall. Colin was a one-time boy wonder of

South Africa Breweries and chair of Wooltru Retailing Group, now in his later years serving as a special consultant for presidents of countries and companies.

Colin had just finished months of exhausting, but ultimately successful work that had brought together dozens of tribal leaders from the Congo to end their warfare and agree on a new constitution. Noting my business school background, he was quick to point out that "the 'head,' the thinking, of the tribal leaders was secondary to their concerns of the heart, their feelings."

"Nothing happens without first establishing trust," Colin continued. "... and that only comes from the heart. So we started by praying together, holding hands, and telling stories about our families. The men smoked cigars together; they drank Johnnie Walker Black [scotch] together. The women learned about each other's children and customs. The result? They became a single family of energized individuals who collectively found ways to transcend language and cultural barriers. And as those barriers fell, so did the political barriers to peace. That's how they ended years of tribal warfare; that's how they were able to establish a new constitution. They even stayed up night after night to get it done. No one ever complained."

It's what I call being of many minds, but *becoming* with one heart.

Involved over the years with Stephen Covey, Colin explained that Covey's *Seven Habits* exemplifies the West's emphasis on "effectiveness" in business. "As Descartes said, 'I think; therefore, I am.' That's the West. Best practices, taxonomies, rules for getting things done more effectively, more efficiently. But what you are missing is something like 'I *feel*; therefore, I am'—the heart, the energy that makes the system go—as I experienced with the Congo tribal leaders."

Foreword

"Ernst and Young recently reported that 66 percent of all strategic decisions don't get implemented. Similarly, we have found that 70 percent of all strategic initiatives are strong in terms of potential 'effectiveness' but have 'low energy' behind them. If you can't capture the 'energy' of an organization through effective teams of impassioned people, nothing happens. At the end of the day, you end up with lots of paper but very little action."

"The source of continuing aliveness is to find your passion and pursue it with whole heart and single mind."

—Gail Sheehy, *New Passages*

So what is passion?

According to filmmaker John Boorman, passion is the "becoming of a person." Are we less of a person, therefore, without passion? Or at the least, should we question what we are doing with the time that has been given us? Is it as Richard Bach of *Jonathan Livingston Seagull* fame hauntingly asked, "You gave your life to become the person you are right now. Was it worth it?"

In my experience with thousands of MBAs and other students of business, their primary challenge is of another sort: Most don't have a clue what they are passionate about! The ways of the world, the rites of what we call "growing up," have left them disconnected from what they cared about as a child, from what might have been nurtured through childhood into adulthood if we lived in a different world. Instead, what might have become a lifetime of passions was locked up long ago in a box in their attic.

Maybe you are one of the lucky ones. You do know. But then you ask yourself, "How can my passion be the basis of a successful career? How can I actually make a living doing things I love? And until I know that, how can I possibly risk giving it a try?"

I facilitate five-day executive retreats that focus on a critical challenge facing a company. Also of importance to senior management, the retreat allows executives to get to know better the "real person" behind each other. When that happens, trust and mutual respect can grow, leading to improved teamwork and expediting implementation efforts in the future. But to do that, we must create a safe environment where the executives feel as comfortable as possible opening up and talking as a whole person to the group.

On Sunday night, I show a film to start our discussion of leadership, teamwork, and the results we hope to see by Friday. I give the executives an "easy" assignment for the next morning to get things started.

Each is asked to prepare a 3- to 5-minute speech to the group about their passion(s). There's only one rule: No talk specifically about family or work. "What you're passionate about may relate to work. You can talk about a hobby, if you wish. Whatever you like," I offer. The truth be told, most spend the entire night in fitful sleep, not sure what they should say the next morning, concerned about how they might look to their peers.

At breakfast the next morning, many will come over to me with comments like, "I hope you don't mind me talking about eating. I love to eat." or "I really do love to play golf. Is that okay?" I know they are nervous, that they are testing me, so I respond with, "Whatever you talk about, make sure you tell us *why* you are so passionate about it."

Tension remains high. Most either don't know what they're passionate about, feel it might be trivial, or are simply afraid to talk about something that they really care about—something that doesn't directly relate to the "safe, acceptable" areas of work or family.

Foreword

We begin. Either a cofacilitator or I go first with a heartfelt speech about a passion deep inside us, often something that springs from our childhood or an emotional experience. Although the first executive to speak might follow with something trite, it rarely happens. The bar—a standard of relevance—has been set.

As the morning moves along, the atmosphere starts to change, almost unnoticed. We share some laughs and some tears. We hear of things like a love for the beauty of nature (and how they miss it by spending all day in their offices), a passion for great books (and how one particularly moved them), or a desire to develop young people (and how they feel when one does well and thanks them).

It is a profound experience. No one leaves the morning session the same as before we started. Even the room feels different. It becomes our primary meeting place, a "home" of sorts, for the next five days. Everyone knows that when they enter this room, truth and openness are now required.

In the next five days, we put together a "passion plan" for each individual, the team, and the organization. We look at their work and the jobs of those who work with them. We ask, "Is the challenge we face because we need people to be more passionate about their jobs, or more jobs people are passionate about?" One thing is clear: Anything done henceforth without passion is not worth doing—organizationally or personally.

> *"Great dancers are not great because of their technique;*
> *they are great because of their passion."*

—*Martha Graham*

Lawler Kang is a man of passion. He is a man who also knows that bringing your passion into your LifeTime (as he calls it) is hard work. It is knowledge that comes from personal experience, from wisdom he earned at nearly the cost of his life.

In return, you have in your hands Lawler's gift to you—a gift that is actually two gifts, two books in one. The first helps you rediscover your passion; the second guides you to put that passion into practicality.

Putting passion into action—figuring out how to do it and then doing it—is a task to be shared with another person or in a group. Why? Like losing weight or ending an addiction, anything that requires you to change not only your attention but also your attitudes and behavior is hard work. And this book is hard work—hard work that offers you the potential of living your life passionately, or as Lawler says, "living a legendary life." So use it in your book club or in your business unit at work. When you do it in a group, working on your plan can even become fun (and at times, funny!).

The personal inspiration of the first few chapters comes from survey data and engaging stories that help you open your mind and heart to the potential of passion. As someone who has faced his own mortality more than once at an early age, Lawler doesn't waste time or mince his words. He shows you how to "rock the boat"—that is, how to find your own way, your own path wide enough to fit just you, based on your individual gifts. He knows how important it is to make every day count. He knows that money is something you give your life energy for—and that it better be a good trade.

What can stop you from reaching out, from really going for it? Lawler raises three issues that are central to my work as well:

- What is money?
- How will you measure success?
- What do you want written on your tombstone?

Foreword

I've found that the two factors that affect people's career choices and patterns most are their relationships with money and with their parents. Real or projected, it doesn't matter—all that matters is their perception of what money is and what their parents think (often transferred to others and society at large) about what is success and a life well lived. These forces can be positive or negative, freeing or controlling. The choice is up to you.

Lawler knows what it is like to have your most fundamental passion tested—your passion for life. He knows what it is like to be told you shouldn't do something, you can't do something, or it is impossible to do something. He also knows what it is like to prove everyone wrong. To this knowledge, he responds powerfully that we only get one chance, not the nine given a cat. He knows that we all have a strength deep inside us—what he calls the core—that cannot be destroyed unless we simply choose not to use it. Lawler challenges each of us to connect with that strength deep inside us and make it real.

Next, you get Lawler's toolkit to guide you in putting together a comprehensive plan. The plan helps ensure that passion happens—and *continues* to happen—throughout your life. Lawler also provides an illustrative case study to make it easy for you to work through your own passions, proficiencies, priorities, plan, and its proof (funding)—his Five Ps of this practical workbook.

In today's economy, if you want to find a job, you have to make a job. Whether you decide to go out on your own or work for someone else, you need to be able to say what it is you want to do, why you can do it well, and how it will add value for your employer or clients. As Lawler notes, "You create your destiny." Bring yourself to market. Turn *your* values into market value. After all, if you don't, who will? If you don't, what will separate you from others offering their services in the marketplace? After all, what makes you different is *you*. *All* of you.

It's important for all of us today to develop this alternate plan. It's not the plan you learned in school, not the plan of past generations, but a plan based on Lawler's tested Five Ps process—a plan that integrates practicality with passion. In the end, you'll discover that passion is not necessarily about doing great things. As Mother Teresa said, "We do no great things; only small things with great love." Instead, passion is about experiencing great love. It's more about being connected to something bigger than yourself, something that brings a bigger spirit and sense of "aliveness" into your life... and beyond.

It has been said that we are all angels with one wing, able to fly only when we embrace each other. I hope you will embrace Lawler and his work. Let him help you take your passion and put it first, ahead of what seems practical—and then make it real. I know it's not easy to do. Or I should say, *was* not as easy to do as it is now. Thanks to Lawler Kang.

> *"When you are inspired by some great purpose... you find yourself in a new, great, and wonderful world. Dormant forces, faculties, and talents become alive, and you discover yourself to be a greater person by far than you ever dreamed yourself to be."*
>
> —*Maharishi Patanjali, founder of yoga*

Dr. Mark S. Albion
Dover, Massachusetts
April 2005

INTRODUCTION

The purpose of this book is to help you constructively rock your boat. Not merely taking a new tack, but simultaneously shivering your hull down to its spine. Why? Because this is your life we are dealing with, not some random project that has gone astray and needs a week or two of concerted effort to regain its bearings. This is your life—its glories, disappointments, promises, and pitfalls—and you only get one. Sure, you can change course and reset your sails as you like. Without stark focus on what truly floats you, though, no matter how strong the winds might blow, your sails will uncontrollably flap disconnected from their purpose, and your internal rigging will hang limp in inconsolable knots. Instinctively, to make real and sustainable change happen, you've gotta clear your holistic decks and start rocking!

The amount of water you take on and the size of waves your pitching might cause is completely up to you and what you think you need. You might produce only a few bathtub ripples and return with a hint of mist on your hair. Or, you might decide to don the nearest life jacket and generate some local surf. Regardless, the relative motion of your ocean and degree of immersion are irrelevant as long as your destination—a safe *and* happy harbor—stays constant. **You** create your destiny. Whatever storms or malevolent currents you encounter, **you** control the time and terms of your life, and you have an innate responsibility to yourself and the world to heed this call, and heed it with passion.

That is precisely the focus of the first four chapters. The stories, the numbers, and the quotes have been collected and presented to roust you from your living slumber as gently, yet as purposefully, as possible. The key point is simple: Each day is a gift, and working your passions is the most productive, least risky, and happiest way to realize this present.

The next six chapters lead you through a tested program called the Process of the Five Ps that uses general business practices to reach three objectives:

- Equip you with the vital triangulation of passions, proficiencies, and priorities that provide practical and salient insights into journeys you can start now and in the future as your circumstances evolve
- Challenge you to contemplate and redefine some basic and critical concepts in a refreshed breeze
- Provide you with a tactical plan and buy-in process to furnish you with the required support to start living in the time of your life

Fundamentally, the process has been built to enable you to realize your dreams. Yes, I believe you can live and even exceed your dreams. However, you **must** treat them as goals and develop realistic plans, replete with milestones and investments of various sorts, to achieve them. Otherwise, they will forever remain "dreams."

The final two chapters prepare you emotionally and financially for what lies ahead. Everything you need to facilitate this change is housed between these covers, notwithstanding writing implements, random scraps of paper, and depending on your preferences, a clunky computer. This said, there is an immense amount of knowledge/power, support, templates, and tools that you can access using the Internet. Please visit www.lawlerkang.com to learn more about how you can harness the power of the Web in working with my process.

One final note: I feel the need to establish a glaring yet often-ignored perspective relating to the essence of this book. The vast majority of you who are reading this book, who **can** read this book, who can even **afford** to buy this book are blessed by "birth luck" as my father-in-law calls it. You have been blessed to have been born into societies whose political and economic systems are relatively stable and advanced, where basic freedoms are taken for granted. You have been raised with an incredible number of advantages over other less fortunate and vast parts of the world, divisions in standards of living that seem to be becoming only more divisive as time goes on. You have by far the greatest ability and opportunity to work your passions and realize your dreams. This is your duty. You are the future of the free markets whose global reach and extraordinary power will only continue to expand. I ask you to heed this call because this is one game we all cannot afford to lose.

CHAPTER 1

WHY DO YOU WORK SO HARD?

A QUESTION OF CONTROL

There is a very good chance you are not living your dreams. In brutal fact, you might not even have tangible dreams to reach. You might be what I call a **scratcher**: someone who fervidly scrapes the system like a chicken, yearning to find that one additional piece of cornmeal to help make the next car payment or nearly delinquent credit card bill. Oh yes, you have dreams; however, your focus on short-term gain and maintaining an ever-escalating standard of living preclude any hope of long-term satisfaction. More specifically, you lack the focus and discipline that will enable you to realize your dreams—dreams that are attainable, but only if you treat them as goals and develop realistic plans to reach them.

Consider one simple question:

Why do you work so hard?

Why do you dedicate so many of your waking and sometimes sleeping hours to your job, often to the cognizant exclusion of friends, family, and other loved ones? For that matter, why did you go to school and work so hard there? Why did you invest (and may still be paying off) anywhere between 20,000 to 200,000 smackers to go to college? Why did you forsake $100,000 or more in lost salary and tuition getting a master's or doctorate, if you chose to go that route?

One primary driver keeps rising to the surface: control. Call it curiosity, competitive spirit, whatever—you want to be able to control how much money you make, your career directions, whom you sleep with at night, where you live, where your kids go to school, and so on and so on. It's amazing to observe the lengths you go to gain merely one or two more slugs of this intuitively uncontrollable concept. At face value, this need for control might not be a bad thing, though digging a little, control can often be a guise for dealing with something you don't understand or you potentially fear—anything from dealing with a smart-mouthed kid to foreign policy. Regardless, this quest for control, if not managed and for the right reasons, can be excruciatingly painful.

UPENDING THE WORK/LIFE BALANCE

A central example of this yearning for control is how you vainly try to balance your time, energy, and focus between the realms of work and life. How **do** you balance your 11.5 hours spent on average per day getting ready, commuting, working, (and commuting again) with your scant bookends of life and time on either side? How **do** you meaningfully interact with your (awake) kids, (not-tired) significant other, and/or (tended to) pets more than a couple hours each day? Can you somehow TiVo your daily cycles, removing all mundane catch-up conversation and chores, to optimally maximize your time? Another way to broach this conundrum is by asking yourself, "Can I leave work and really leave it?" You can't just enter the Dark and Gloomy Cave of Work and then return to the Bright and Blissful Garden of Life as it suits you.

In this context, the implied metaphor of a balancing scale casts work in an inappropriate light. If work wins, life loses? Or if life wins, work loses? **HUH**? Is work such a **BAD** thing? Perhaps if you perceive your means of income as merely a job, then yes,

BRING IN THE SCALES, and make sure your life-side weights are nice and heavy to really piss you off as you watch the space of time collapse around every ticking second as your daily grind comes to a close. Yes, the term **work** has certain connotations: a degree of difficulty, of challenge, and even sacrifice. It also implies achievement, advancement, and fundamentally something noble. How could our society and standard of living ever improve without work—impassioned work at that? Have you ever heard people describe what they do as "my life's job"? No. Portraying your commitment as "my life's work" carries a decidedly different nuance. The sooner you can approach what your life's work might be, the sooner you can leave that absurd and undefeatable balance behind.

The fact is that balance is not possible. Maybe it is if you believe in multiple dimensions or other breaks in our quantum time fabric, but from my humble perspective, balancing just doesn't work. Work is an integral part of life, not a weighty counterbalance to it. You should love your work with the same passion as you love life! Imagine your boss casually sitting you down in the lunchroom one day to discuss your recent spate of late and tortured office nights and then screaming at you, "You idiot—It's all life!" The secret to upending the balance is upending your perspective on how you deal with its working parts. Being able to apply the same impassioned perspective to both work and life will moot your scale metaphor in a heartbeat.

Let's banish the term "balance" from your daily vernacular and replace it with **priority**—work/life priority. Balancing is how circus performers entertain. The success of your acts—work, pastimes, kids, and so on—is driven by prioritizing how you want to spend the time of your life, your **LifeTime** as I will call it for the remainder of this book. Yes, time is money, but infinitely more important, time is life. Although this distinction between balance and priority is subtle in nature, after you adopt it, its implications on how you look at, structure, and execute your life can be extraordinarily profound.

Ask yourself this baseline question:

Am I having The Time of My Life, in the Time of My Life?

Don't worry if your answer lacks enthusiasm. This is a tough nut to crack. The concept of being able to autonomously live your life has unfortunately been under sustained attack for quite some time because so much of your tactical day and night have been signed away to others. Following are piddly examples, but combined, they make a point. Have you ever read, word for word, the back of your credit card statement? Your home, car, or life insurance policy? How about your benefits package at work? Rental or mortgage contracts? Investment prospectuses? Any piece of legislation—local, state, or federal? Can you even begin to understand those insurance Description of Benefits statements? No? Well, why not? This is potentially important stuff, no?

How about something more general? Ever thought about understanding the terms and conditions of "Keeping up with the Joneses"? You must have wondered at some point why you need to own that newest model import car, need to possess the latest whiz-bang piece of technology, need to eat at the trendiest restaurants whose names you cannot hope to pronounce, and need to send your kids to preschools costing upward of 50 times what the average global citizen earned last year? Call it curiosity, competitive spirit, whatever. Are you happy with these terms? Fundamentally, do you think you can win a game whose rules are seemingly beyond your control?

Living in our society implicitly requires the need to negotiate with other people's terms, terms that can readily engulf you, rendering you a passive participant in the sport of life. You have been explicitly (or worse, implicitly) contractualized to the point where you don't even care to know the provisions of whatever transaction you need to make. "The last four digits of my social security number are 3491. Just give me the pen. Where do I need to initial and sign?"

You need to live life on your terms.

WHERE ARE YOU?

You might like your work but not love it. You could be one of the 75 percent who responded to a *Forbes* poll as being "unfulfilled" and "unhappy" with their jobs. You could be one of the roughly 30 percent who responded in outright negative terms—"I hate my job . . . If it weren't for the paycheck, I'd leave tomorrow." You might be living the worst possible atrocity: relegating your own needs beyond the back burner to work an unhappy job to survive in a jungle of terms you dislike and can't control. Worst of all, there isn't an off ramp or even a signpost on the horizon, and your spiritual gas tank's warning light is starting to flicker. Don't you ever just want to murmur, declare, or scream at the world, "Stop, I'm getting off!"?

So. . . what is holding you back?

Why are you hesitant to change, try something new and possibly different, figure out what really lights your happy lamp, and then work like a campaigning politician to make it burn? Isn't success simply loving your work and life with the same degree of passion?

I'd like to share a story that highlights why you should start thinking about these questions and how they might start to impact your journey . . . **NOW**!

CHAPTER 2

WE AREN'T CATS

YOUR CORE OF STEEL

I was 14, and the world was my oyster: freshman class president, co-captain of the JV football team, sports editor of the yearbook, and making decent grades at a competitive private high school in Southern California. I was training for a marathon, had taken up surfing, was an avid skateboarder, and had enrolled in a local martial arts program. I was also on track to becoming an Eagle Scout in the Boy Scouts of America in near record time. Although my parents were living apart, life was pretty darn sweet. In literally a heartbeat, a minute weakness in a particular cell wall would dramatically change all this forever.

I collapsed during a football game with a Grand Mal seizure and woke to find no sensation below my waist. I was rushed to the hospital where I was eventually diagnosed with a neural aneurysm. Aneurysms are basically weak arterial walls, which expand like balloons and often burst. They can happen in your heart or your brain; mine was in the latter. The pain was unbearable, and any sensation—light, sound, and so on—triggered another blast. Surviving both the initial trauma (more than half of us die within a month of rupture) and surgery without experiencing permanent paralysis, mental retardation, or loss of a faculty is rare—less than 10 percent.

The operation lasted eight hours, during which the blood supply to my brain needed to be shut off for almost four minutes in order to properly clip off the balloon. I was in a coma for three days post-op and awoke with slurred speech, deficiencies in my right side (much like people who have strokes), and looking like the Elephant Man. The left side of my head had swollen to the size of a honeydew melon, eclipsing my left eye. When the swelling subsided and the eye opened, my eyeball was stuck in the outside corner, requiring tedious and blurry exercises to regain synchronicity. Rehabilitation to be functionally walking, talking, and seeing again would require a total of nine months. Sometime during my two-week hospital stay, my parents told me their separation of four years was going to be final. The divorce required an additional two years to complete.

I was mad and jealous of the world. One moment I was running Cloud Nine ragged, and the next, I was disfigured and wheelchair bound. I revolted, started listening to punk rock, and indulged in many of the existential pleasures that define Los Angeles. I didn't drop out of school, though. Something inside me told me to keep going, that there was a reason all this stuff was happening to me. I applied and was accepted to college. Things were looking up—I had worked myself back into decent physical shape, was skiing and riding bikes with helmets, was body boarding, had a girlfriend, and felt fairly confident in my ability to take on the demands of the next big step. May 15, 1985 tried its best to change this.

※

I was hiking with my senior high school class in Arizona when I doubled over on the trail with an intense pain in my stomach. A day and a half later, I was airlifted straight to surgery, where the doctors reported that if I hadn't arrived in the next couple of hours,

I surely would have died. This diagnosis was a Meckles Diverticulum, an outgrowth from the inside wall of my colon, which basically backs everything up. The attending physician remarked that this was the first case of this particular dysfunction he had seen in 25 years of practice. I spent the next four weeks in the Flagstaff hospital on morphine, with tubes protruding from virtually every orifice in my body. I lost about 3 feet of my colon, gained 17 staple scars in my abdomen, and watched 30 pounds of muscle disappear. I also developed a pollinoidal cyst, a deep sore on the tip of my tailbone triggering excruciating pain with virtually any body movement. Thankfully, I was going to college. Pale and frail but still determined, I graduated from high school.

My first two years at college were absolutely phenomenal. I rebuilt my body, was doing decently well in my studies, and was looking forward to spending a semester in Japan.

Then, in May 1987, the stomach war drums started pounding again. My sister checked me into a hospital near Boston, and the next morning, I was opened up again. Another three weeks of morphine, immobility, sucking, breathing and urinating through plastic, another loss of 30 pounds and another 17 staples later, I found myself on a plane bound back to LA with a small tube protruding from my stomach to prevent my colon from closing around the procedure.

A couple of days later, the tube (which was actually six feet long) was carefully removed, and I breathed a long, long sigh of relief. "That last one almost killed me," I can remember thinking. My mind immediately started focusing on the future—the arduous process of rebuilding my body and preparing to go to Japan. That night, however, the deep thumping of my internal artillery once again started firing. The morning of June 7, 1987, for the third time in two years, I found myself counting down from 100 for the anesthesiologist. The ensuing 24-day stay reminded me of the scene from *A Clockwork Orange* when the lead character is tied to his seat, eyes held open to view repugnant scenes of violence. In this version, my Demerol-drenched attention was transfixed solely on the simple, stark, and unsettling questions, "Why am I here?" The veins in my hands collapsed from the IVs, so they started attaching the tubes to my feet.

It was then, in my darkest hour, when I realized that deep inside each of us lies a core of unbreakable, unalterable steel—passion, life, or whatever else you want to call it. Some meet it but for unfortunate reasons choose not to interact. Those who have embraced it or who can even merely **acknowledge** it can become unstoppable. What's more, I realized that by believing in one's core, that petty, smoke-and-mirror figure called fear can be unmasked for what it really is—**nothing**. I must shorten Franklin D. Roosevelt's famous line a bit, "There is nothing to fear. Period!" Armed with this new resolve and the conviction that the only thing that ultimately could bring me down was myself, I decided to give this "future" thing one more try.

Once again, I started the long process of rebuilding my body. I made it to Japan, which was an extraordinary experience. I wrote a thesis, graduated from college, and got a job working for a Japanese firm, starting as a glorified shipping clerk. Two years later, I was earning three times my starting salary, and with some assistance from my father, I bought a townhouse half a block from the beach in Venice, California. I also started an import-export firm out of Yogyakarta, Indonesia. Three years later, after burning out of both pursuits, I was accepted to the MBA program at the Wharton School of the University of Pennsylvania, where my studies of entrepreneurial management led me to found an Internet business (before they were called dot-coms). I subsequently ran numbers for Nortel's acquisition of Bay Networks, worked in an Internet incubator, and then joined another consulting firm called Scient, as an engagement manager in the business unit focused on venture capital funded start-ups. Scient was a leading force in the eBusiness boom, at its height boasting a market cap that exceeded $9 billion. I was then promoted to managing director of Northeast operations and established and grew the Boston practice. I have since been fortunate to be able to help the employees of four failing technology companies try to turn their boats around.

By all accounts, my career path has been a bit serendipitous. Peering through the lenses of passion, it all makes perfect sense, although while I was in the throes of the moment(s), figuring out *where* I was going and more importantly *why* seemed to be one of those mystical and cloudy secrets that only years of psychoanalytical hypnosis could coax out of me.

I would like to expand on six themes from my story to set a high-level context for approaching the daunting task of figuring out your direction in life. These six concepts are the best reflective realizations of the joy I experience when waking up and simply being able to walk, talk, eat, and see without assistance. Take them for what they are worth to you; they are worth a LifeTime to me!

1. WE AREN'T CATS!

You don't get nine lives. All you get is ONE shot to take this thing called life by the tail, swing it around your head a couple of times, and say, "Listen up, partner, I am going to milk you for ALL you can give me, starting NOW!" Have you ever heard people say, "Oh, he was only 50; he was so young when he had his seizure." Or "She is 45; she is still so young." What a farce! They are typically younger than the people who are referring to them, but they are *NOT* young. People seem to correlate youth with the power of promise, the ability to change the world, make your fortunes, and so on before you get dragged down into those dank caves of conformity from which no one can escape. You should be young at heart, no doubt, although projecting youth relative to your own age is simply (and vainly) trying to escape the inevitable. You aren't a cat. Let's milk this trip!

2. BELIEVE IN YOUR CORE

It's frightening to observe the strength of the human race. Think back merely a couple hundred years, before vaccines, modern capitalism and democracy, and yes, even before e-mail. The relative amount of misery your ancestors had to endure compared with your top ten reasons for therapy is like comparing ten grand invested in Berkshire Hathaway stock in 1965 and what it would be worth today. Your strength, your courage, and your indomitable spirit have not vanished; they merely have been dressed up in fashionable attire, immunized, and regard a cross-town cab ride of more than 15 minutes as abhorrent. Your core will **always** be there for you when and if you need it. Fortunately, you don't need to endure my melodrama to realize its existence. Just know it's there, silently waiting inside you, the most powerful force in the universe, which can surmount **whatever** obstacles are thrown your way. You are already unstoppable.

I'd like to reference an outstanding book authored by Jim Collins and crew called *Good to Great*, which both underscores and adds a critical nuance to this observation. Per the title, the book explores factors separating merely good companies from great ones by looking at shareholder returns over 30-year periods. In breaking down the managerial aspects of great companies, many of which faced severe adversarial scenarios, Collins uncovered a repeating theme in the way their management perceived the world. He termed it the **Stockdale Paradox**.

Vice Admiral James Stockdale was the highest-ranking U.S. armed forces personnel captured in the Vietnam War. Imprisoned for 8 years in the Hanoi Hotel and enduring 20 rounds of torture, he never broke. Why? "Because you have to believe that no matter how bad things get, no matter what the odds might seem to be, you must believe that you will prevail." It's as simple as that. This one belief carried him through situations that make my ordeal look like a Sunday walk in the park overdosed on Prozac.

The paradox enters when Collins inquired which of his fellow prisoners broke. "The optimists," Stockdale immediately replied. Huh? Here you are extolling the virtues of a positive mental attitude, and now you are saying it will kill you? Not quite. The optimists, according to Stockdale, were those who would set a mental expectation that they would be released by next Easter, or next Christmas, and when these arbitrary milestones came and passed, they lost it. Rather, Stockdale counterbalances his winning belief by taking a cold, hard look at the facts of your situation and using them to drive your decision-making processes, aiming for "True North," as some consultants like to call it. If you want returns from this investment of your LifeTime, you **must** accept and use both sides of the Stockdale Paradox. You will prevail, but only if you are starkly honest with where you are. In essence, you must understand your reality in order to change your reality.

3. Accept X-Factors

This X has two meanings: the usual "air of mystery," but also an abbreviated form of **exogenous**, or things that happen outside of your realm of control—forces that, for no apparent rhyme or reason, can alter the direction of your life forever. We all live under a thick layer of X-Factors, which we fail (or perhaps more appropriately, fear) to see. The fascinating thing about X-Factors is that they can be good just as often as they can be bad. Think of them as Chance cards from the game Monopoly; sometimes you go directly to jail, sometimes you get a windfall, and other times you are sent to a particular property that can be cheap or expensive, depending on who owns it. The critical part of this metaphor is that chance is in control here, not you!

You could be sunning yourself on some random beach and ask your future spouse to oil your back. You could be sunning yourself on some random beach and bump into an old acquaintance who is looking for a person with your assets in your dream city. You could be sunning yourself on some random beach and find yourself running for your life from a 30-foot wall of water. You simply cannot know. Your future is unwritten.

A brilliant depiction of the pervasive nature of X-Factors can be seen in the plot of the movie *Sliding Doors*, starring Gwyneth Paltrow. The same person's life is split and then tracked as it continues from the daily happenstance of making or missing a subway train. This one random X-Factor triggers a multitude of cascading events with a range of emotional results. Reflect on your life to date. Have there been any coincidental connections that have had major implications on your life? Here are a few examples:

- A friend of your father's knew someone who helped you get the job of your dreams, but only by happening to overhear a conversation about you.
- A fellow traveler you kept in touch with introduced you to your current significant other.

- A friend from summer camp whom you bumped into while on a business trip talked you into moving to her city.

The connections and possibilities quickly become impossible to fathom. "What if I were to have a conversation with that person I saw at the park? I wonder where that would have led?" "What if I were to apply for that job that lies squarely in my passion zone, even though my résumé does not seem to support me?" "What if I ran late to the office because I needed to pick up my shoes?"

Do you know anyone who was lost in 9/11? It was a sparkling late summer morning. Perhaps that person was thinking, "I need to get the kids to school on time, prep for the 11 o'clock conference call with a client, change my 401(k) investment allocations because I think the market has hit bottom, and pick up the dry cleaning this afternoon…"

… and whammo, literally out of the blue…

- 2,819 people were gone.
- 1,609 friends were without spouses or a partner.
- 3,051 children were without a parent.

A colleague from the New York Scient office was on the 110th floor when the first plane hit. My wife's then-employer did a huge amount of business with Cantor-Fitzgerald, which lost 658 employees, or roughly 85 percent of their headquarters' staff. I worked two blocks from Ground Zero for a spell in 2002, and my morning walk through Tribeca would take me by the thick, black-iron fences of St. John's Church, adjacent to the emptiness, where pictures of loved ones fluttered in the breeze—grim reminders of a tragic and real X-Factor at play.

Events like 9/11 and the Sumatra tsunami spotlight this point: No matter how in control you might perceive yourself as being, forces that are way beyond your individual ability to influence or avert can randomly cause incredible amounts of both harm and joy. Having a B.A., B.S., J.D., M.D., R.N., M.B.A., C.F.A., C.P.A., Ph.D., or even a high-paying job at a top-tier monolith can't protect you from these expressions of chaos. I absolutely despise that utterly presumptuous and obnoxious question that litters everyone's interview list: "So, where do you see yourself in five years?" Those who believe in crystal balls should be prepared to eat glass.

So how should you deal with this modified "invisible hand"? First, don't try to control it because you will inevitably go insane trying. Rather, be open and ready to deal with the bad events, and exploit the good ones when they happen—because sooner or later, they *are* going to happen! Let me be clear. I am not necessarily saying that you should drop everything and buy every insurance policy imaginable. It is a state of awareness I am driving toward here—an awareness of the potential for amazing good and horrific bad that pre-empts us every day. At life's barest level, this is what the second half of the Stockdale Paradox—facing the unalterable facts—is all about.

This state of awareness was recently highlighted by actress Sharon Stone, who in 2001 coincidentally also had a brain aneurysm. It took doctors 11 days to stop her blood flow. She survived. Her father was then diagnosed with cancer and given a 3-percent chance of survival. They both survived. Then Sharon's marriage dissolved. By this point, she could survive anything. "Sometimes I think if we are awake, life traumas are a gift," she said. "Your life needs to change, and you come out of it a different person."

I couldn't agree more.

4. What's Your Point?

Where is your limit? What will it take for you to acknowledge you are not living on your terms? When will you realize you are **not** having the time of your life, in the time of your life. When will you understand that life is fleeting and there are other maps to guide your boat? Will it be an X-Factor of some extreme proportion? A relative or good friend's death? An accident while tootling off to the store? Will it be having a glimpse of how the world might remember you? Will it be something as seemingly benign as a random news story you hear, which unleashes years of pent-up anguish and frustration of working for the machine? Or could it just be getting older and the innate understandings that accompany LifeTime and experiences?

I am amazed at how much abuse we humans can bear. We endure years of knowing, "This job isn't right for me," "I don't get along well with my boss," or "I hate this cursed commute." We have forgotten that we can control these and other sources of duress. We experience years of seeing our most important and valuable asset being destroyed right before our eyes and feeling helpless to stop it.

Donna Modica provides an excellent example of someone who reached her point. Donna was climbing the ladder at one of Boston's larger financial institutions. She was lured by the power, the money, and the need to make more money to help her family live their dreams. Yet the higher she climbed and the more responsibilities she accepted, the more constrained she felt, particularly in terms of her time. No matter how disciplined and organized, she found herself staying at the office later and later. Her point came when her daughter called her at work at 9 p.m. to ask her when she was going to come home to help her with a project for school that was due tomorrow. Donna started crying. This was the straw. Donna realized that her priorities had to change, money be damned!

Donna subsequently resigned and has since gone into career counseling, working in the career development office at the Carroll School of Business at Boston College. She recounts, "Yes, the initial money drop was difficult to deal with, but we were able to work things out much easier than I had originally figured. The trade-off though, in terms of being able to spend time with my kids, has been phenomenal and frankly priceless. I can always go back to the corporate world if I want, but for now, I am very happy."

I am sure you have heard many similar stories about people who burn out or reach their point. The term "going postal" describes an unfortunate and extremely bad case of this syndrome. What's **your** point?

5. WHATEVER YOU DO (IN LIFE), DO IT WITH PASSION

At the end of the day, the day is over. Wake up, work out, commute, work, commute, spend time with kids and friends, make dinner, wash dishes, watch TV, coordinate tomorrow, sleep. You can't go back. There are no rewind capabilities, no TiVo, no second chances. You can start only from where you stopped today, and who knows what tomorrow might bring. The legendary Jim Morrison sung it best, "The future's uncertain, and the end is always near." This insight is blatantly obvious, yet you probably tend to shy away from it for reasons of social acceptability, lack of convenience, lack of income potential, or a thousand other trumped-up rationales.

Why not approach all facets of your LifeTime with the power of your passion? What do you really have to lose when you can gain so much?

You can hedge investments, but do you want to hedge life?

6. What Do You Want Your Tombstone to Say?

This is one of those rare things you really can control. Think a moment about what your answer might be. Imagine having the gift of premonition and knowing your day is coming much sooner than you had planned. How do you want the world to remember you? Having difficulties with your epitaph? You are not alone. In fact, the vast majority of the U.S. workforce—hell, the entire world—would find answering this question a bit difficult.

The innate power of this question can be illustrated by the actions of two legendary, but quite real people. The first is Laurence Rockefeller. Laurence was born into one of the world's largest family fortunes, but he chose a notably different path from his political and banking siblings. In college, he studied philosophy and, per *The New York Times*, "long wrestled with the question of how he might most efficiently and satisfyingly use the great wealth into which he was born." This soul searching early on in life resulted in some extraordinary accomplishments rooted in his passion for the wilderness and conservation. He assisted with, or created outright, many of America's most treasured national parks, including Redwood National Park in California and Grand Teton National Park in Wyoming. He also spawned the eco-tourism craze when he funded the first series of environmentally friendly hotels. Over his lifetime, Rockefeller donated more than

$500 million to various philanthropic efforts. He said, "I profoundly feel that the art of living is the art of giving. You are fulfilled in the moment of giving, of doing something beyond yourself."

Although Laurence's financial resources dwarf yours, there is no correlation between the scale of giving and the art of living, and I'd wager the fulfillment you receive from your own philanthropic endeavors vastly outweighs whatever you gave in the process. In this context, giving could be one of the best conceivable investments of your LifeTime. Imagine the impact the strength of your impassioned core and its ability to generate a legacy of lucre of all sorts—money, love, kindness, and so on—could have on the world.

"Yes, he did great things," you say to yourself. "But he never had to worry about making the next house payment." Very true, and to be fair, most of us (with very rare exception) won't be able to replicate his financial capabilities. This said, you have one fundamental thing in common with this Rockefeller. You wrestle, on a daily basis I would argue, with the question of how you might most efficiently and satisfyingly use the great wealth of **life** into which you have been born. Your time on this earth is by far the most valuable asset you have at your disposal. It is how you choose to allocate your LifeTime that determines what your tombstone will say.

The second story relates to Alfred Nobel, founder of the Nobel Peace Prize. Any idea what Nobel's initial claim to fame was? He owned the patent for the production of nitroglycerin—dynamite—the most powerful force on the planet at the time. This monopoly bestowed him with an immense fortune over the course of his LifeTime.

There is some debate as to what caused Alfred to bequeath his entire estate to "those who, during the preceding year, shall have conferred the greatest benefit on mankind." One hypothesis is that he was able to read his own obituary due to the mistaken identity of his brother, who was killed in a freak factory explosion. Extensive research in the Parisian archives does not corroborate this story, however. Others conjecture that a woman close to him might have influenced his apparent desire to be remembered for something far more lasting (and beneficial?) than the production of dynamite. No one knows precisely why and when Alfred made his decision; the important thing is that he was able to make it in the time of his life. You will never know how the world will remember you unless you, like Alfred, take up the responsibility of generating a life worthy of remembrance.

This story is fitting for another reason. You, like Alfred, have been given the ability over the course of your LifeTime to touch hundreds, thousands, and even millions of your fellow human beings by how you choose to prioritize and allocate your LifeTime. The ever-expanding need for business to become involved in all levels and functions of our society enhances this capability, yet simultaneously calls for leaders everywhere to step up and **passionately** take part in creating a better world for us all. It doesn't matter if you are a CEO, office administrator, book-keeper, flight attendant, technician, accountant, or parent. Your tombstone can be **extraordinarily** important!

ONE FINAL THOUGHT

I'd like to close this chapter by sharing some remarks left to us by someone diagnosed with Amyotrophic Lateral Sclerosis (ALS). ALS is one of the worst conditions you could ever imagine con-tracting. Roughly 50 percent of those afflicted die within two years of diagnosis, and the vast majority of the remaining half go within five years. ALS basically paralyzes your muscles, eventually making movement of any type—walking, speaking, or even blinking your eyes—impossible, although your brain remains completely lucid and intact. Though ALS predominantly strikes men in their later years, it can rear its Medusa-like head to anyone, at any time. There are no known cures or even therapies that can significantly extend life longer than a couple of months. One moment you are strapping and happy with a shimmering future ahead, and the next, you have been issued a death sentence.

Will Hubben was such a spirit, and post-diagnosis, he became a leading figure in the ALS crusade, developing a weekly e-mail information update read religiously by 1,300 researchers, clinicians, and patients looking to beat this horrid disease. He edited it himself until his death in May 2004. The following words, written by Will in 2002, summarize the essence of this chapter better than anything else I could ever hope to find.

> I have ALS now. That is my condition. Some people are born blind or severely disabled, or into starving poverty, or are in prison because of their beliefs. Life is a gift of joy and love, but also of pain and loss. I'll take it however it comes.
>
> Accepting that things are just the way they are allows me to make the best of a difficult situation. Nobody expects to live forever. ALS might kill me, but it might not. I don't get to decide the moment or nature of my death. I only get to decide how I live, given my conditions.
>
> We all have the capacity to love and be loved, to grow closer to whatever god(s) we are into, to simply enjoy the company of others, to feel sunshine on our faces, to see the incredible world of nature, to listen to a fascinating

multicultural world full of music and stories. When is it not enough? I'm glad that all I have is ALS, that all these things are still available to me. I can't backpack anymore, or sea kayak, or dress and feed myself, but I am experiencing joy in my life. It's still me inside. And I used to think I couldn't be happy without those things.

CHAPTER 3

WHAT IS THE END GAME?

WHAT IS MONEY?

Let me start off by making a blatant observation: It is hard in any society, ours in particular, not to have a certain level of income. Money can buy you education, a nice house, sporty clothes, a shmancy car, and vacations to far-away places. **If money talks, it can also lie.** Money can provide temporary material satisfaction, which studies show can quickly become an endless loop of wanting more and more. It can trap you into an ever-increasing number of monthly "fixed" expenses, it can't buy love, and it makes the process of divorce downright miserable for everyone involved.

Money, people say, buys you time and freedom, although this begs the question, "Whose time and freedom was it in the first place?" It was yours, of course, which makes this statement patently silly and underlines an important point: Money, standing naked and alone, is not a bad thing. Rather, it is the quest for money, our societal focus on this quest, and the consequent correlation of success with money that has turned this neutral concept into a raging demon, a machine you must constantly feed lest it consume you. If taken in this context, what is money buying you time and freedom from? From the quest for money, of course! Or, from a recent perspective, the increases in control you study and work so hard to gain are being negated by this same quest for control.

Having more money can buy you an even nicer house, an even shmancier car, and nicer vacations. Mind you, desiring a particular lifestyle is not a bad concept per se, and generating lots of money is similarly not intrinsically bad or evil. It is the process, mindset, and definition of success you adopt in the pursuit of these objectives that I'd like to focus on because all three, sooner than later, will start cheating your real end game: being happy.

Following are vignettes of some folks who have taken the bold step of following a path less trodden. I invite you to look for a pattern or two relating to how they have defined their success. Although these characters come from and are going to all walks of life, they share a fundamental bond: the realization that they wanted to live on their terms.

VIRGINIA

My daughter loves to create art, and one of her favorite places to do so is the Coastal Arts Works, owned by a woman named Virginia, about a half-mile jaunt from our house. The weathered building has a cozy, warm, inviting feeling, accentuated by her yellow Labrador, Ridge, who is either exuberantly licking anyone who comes through the door or has passed out on his couch. Once a consultant, always a consultant, I was curious to know the economics of her business and, passion hat on, why and how she got into starting and running a pottery shop. As my older hoodlum was scouring the unfinished animals, plates, and mugs looking for something to consecrate, I sat down with Virginia over a pot of herbal tea.

"How did I get into this?" she laughed. "Well, I studied art history and architecture in college but then realized what I really wanted to do was teach children art. So I got my master's in education and tried out a stint in the public schools. What a disappointment that was! First, the politics in schools are outrageous. Second, though, I quickly realized that "art" classes in public schools, if they have them at all, consisted of a rolling cart that stopped in your classroom for 45 minutes and then went on. How can you teach kids about the creative process in a variety of mediums in 45 minutes in a stale classroom? Public schools were not for me."

She continued, "I had studied pottery in high school and had loved it. In an instant, I knew what my next step would be—THIS," motioning around the main room inhabited by four splattered spinning wheels, a kiln, a large table for everyone to work on, various finished things for sale, and a battered, legless couch adjacent to a small TV. A shelf above the table has the words *Be Creative* painted on the wall, and all the *E*s are potted plants. "Where else can you go, take as much time as you'd like, learn and create things, and have fun doing it?" she rhetorically asked.

"What about the economics of this business. Is this profitable?" I inquired.

"Oh, there are months when I don't make the rent on this place," she replied matter-of-factly. "I mean, everyone thought I was crazy to go out, rent 2,000 square feet of space, and open up shop. I'd have to say the whole task was pretty daunting. I had to write a business plan and approach banks for money." The closing of that sentence was uttered with a tone of empathetic disdain. "In fact, though, I didn't need their money. My father lent me some, which was matched by my mother-in-law," she proudly continued, "and I have been here for four years."

"But what is most important is that I *absolutely* love what I am doing. I leap out of bed at 6:30 and can't wait to get here. I love to throw clay, and I love teaching kids and adults how to throw. At Christmas time, I will open at 8 a.m., and before I know it, it is already 6 p.m. My husband sometimes needs to call me at 11 at night just to make sure I'm okay... People will come to me and say, 'Wow, how did you create this? I have always thought about starting my own business.' I always tell them, 'Just do it!' "

Virginia's passion is infectious, and it is leading her to some potentially interesting financial rewards in addition to life returns. She has been able to network her way into some of Boston's finest golf and yacht clubs with ceramic cigar holders, emblazoned with the club's respective crest. Her aim is to own all such clubs east of the Rockies, and with her passion and product, she could very well be on her way to hitting pay-clay. Go, Virginia!

EDDIE

Eddie is a friend from trade school. I hadn't seen him for at least five years, and I recently bumped into him at a mutual friend's wedding in Northern California. I had been hearing snippets about Eddie's "successes" over time. He had apparently become a fairly big shot in the media world, doing mergers and acquisitions and corporate venture capital for a large media company. Our conversation quickly centered on the wacky and twisty nature of our careers to date. His pursuits had made him relocate a few times, and then a few more. "I had just settled in the Midwest and had actually bought a house there when the decision was made to consolidate some of the properties, so I returned to California." "This jacket," he continued with a tired smile and equally as weary gesture, "is the only nice piece of clothing that isn't crated up someplace."

But here was the really interesting thing: A passion for bicycle racing was taking over his operating system. He had started a little company—www.velo-fit.com—advising competitive racers on how to prepare for and win races. His eyes, glassy and fatigued while recounting the complex chains of his corporate exploits, suddenly became lively and warm. His posture improved, his arms animated. "You know the best thing about this business? I can ride **every** day!" he beamed as though a spotlight had just picked him up as he was mounting the winner's platform to accept his Gold

Happy Medal at the Life Olympics. It was clear to me that Eddie was making some major changes to his term sheet. Where this business could go is worthy of discussion; however, an even larger and more important question seems to have been answered: Eddie understands the drivers of his success.

JULES

Julie, or Jules to most, is another classmate from graduate school. Jules is a fun-loving, entrepreneurial Type A poster girl whose Southern accent has been able to withstand more than 10 years of speaking above the Mason-Dixon line. Jules did her summer internship at American Express, although it proved to her that the corporate world is not cut out for her.

Jules got involved as VP of marketing in a retail start-up that produced both branded and customized baseball hats. I always loved hearing stories about both her creative ways of spreading her company's word and the tactical snafus that plague all small and growing concerns. Handing out bumper stickers that arrived literally hot off the presses at a professional football game was a favorite anecdote of hers. However, I could tell that even though she was learning a ton and having some fun, the full scope of her passion was not being utilized. Eventually, she left the company and did some Internet marketing consulting for a spell. "It paid the bills, but it also wasn't my calling," I remember her saying.

Then one day in the mail, I got a postcard announcing the grand opening of Jules Place, sub-themed "Art for the Living." Jules' real passion, it turns out, is art. Not creating it per se, but admiring it and helping others enjoy it. She also realized that there was a need for someone to represent up-and-coming artists with up-and-coming price points. She had shopped for retail space on some of Boston's main footways, but the numbers simply wouldn't work out. That was discouraging at first but then became a blessing. Jules thought to herself, "Hell, I love art, and I love people... This business is my passion. My tag line combines art and life. Why not make my gallery a part of my home?" And that is precisely (and tastefully) what she did. She tore down walls, installed enough wiring to circle a football field, hung lights, stocked her bar, and was ready for business! Although the going was slow initially, her client base and reputation for providing exceptional art at reasonable prices started to ramp up.

Jules has since been featured in the *Wall Street Journal* and was on the cover of *The Boston Globe*'s magazine. She is now tinkering with her model and has expanded her wares geographically into adjacent states. Her Web site is www.JulesPlace.com and I wish I had more wall space to accommodate some of her finds! "Yes, there are down days, and it is hard running your own business. You need the discipline of a saint. This said, I couldn't be happier coming home every day or working in an environment where I am surrounded by an ever-changing display of art that I love!" Jules is well on her way, and her success metrics are obvious.

SHORT CLIPS

Then there is the story of the Stanford Business School graduate who gave up being a consulting slave, moved to a ski resort, opened a small financial planning shop, and skis 125+ days per year. Her parents were aghast. What on earth was their bright and motivated daughter doing wasting her talents waiting for the first flakes to fall when there were empires to build? From my outlier point of view, I'd say whatever investment had been made in their daughter's education has yielded outstanding returns since she realized both *how* she'd like to define her successes in life *and* how to attain them. On top of this, who knows where her business will take her?

What Is the End Game?

One of my sister's former roommates shared a story about a recently christened OB/GYN practitioner with whom she had worked during her residency. His life was far over in the fast track. Not even the "Okay-to-speed-carpool" lane would suffice as he frantically tried to keep his practice, marriage, and new kids together. Finally, one day he realized that whatever financial gains and capabilities he was trying so hard to create simply weren't worth the cost (the $270 fines for breaking the carpool lane's rules being a small factor in this calculation). He reduced his hours, rebudgeted his finances, and slowed down his life to a speed that he could control. Initially, the money part was difficult for his family, although they quickly realized the gains in his demeanor, spirit, and sanity more than offset these temporary losses. Nowadays, he leisurely obeys the speed limit and is reportedly so happy, rested, and satisfied that former colleagues have a difficult time identifying him. When he is ready to increase his hours, he can.

Finally, there is the Wharton graduate who left a Big Four consulting behemoth to pursue his real love—being a personal trainer. Yep, that's right. He traded in his Armani suits and Cole Hahn shoes for sweats and cross-trainers. Imagine the look on the gym manager's face when he reviewed this gentleman's resume! Who knows where his journey will take him! I'd bet wherever it goes, the fact that he is happy will carry him farther than he ever thought possible.

It might seem that I am cherry-picking my examples from some hard-working, fortunate, and accomplished folks. You might not have wanted or been able to endure the gauntlet of college and graduate school, which is **not** a bad thing. In fact, to reiterate, one could argue that those of you who did not forsake the average American mortgage in lost salary and tuition merely to hang another scrap of paper on your wall have more confidence than those (myself included) who needed the comfort or boost of the additional degree. There are some incredibly valuable aspects of such experiences, particularly the network of people you can access. The fact remains, though, that a large part of the reason why you go to school is to gain the confidence to be able to control the world through understanding more of it.

This noted, consider again what these gifted folks are doing with their hard-earned diplomas—throwing clay, coaching racers, selling art, and working out. Hmmm… Do you think **you** could compete in those pursuits without such high-powered training? How much of their studies do you think they are using on a daily basis? What is keeping you from trusting your gut when it would appear that their years of study have blatantly overqualified them and are arguably now tangential to their working life? In a funny sense, they might have needed to compete in a particular arena to understand that they didn't want or quite possibly need to compete in that arena.

A markedly interesting question arises in this context: To what extent did their pursuit of more parchment, corporate bliss, or academic prowess actually **hold them back** from realizing their callings? At a deeper and more pressing level, how much of their LifeTime did they commit to these processes that might have been better spent accelerating the identification and initiation of their respective journeys? Conversely, did they need the ordeal to realize what is truly important to them? Life is an iterative process, although you get only one life to spin.

A MADNESS OF METHOD?

Were you able to notice any patterns from these stories? Across all examples, the subjects implicitly defined their criteria or metrics for success by defining the direction of their journeys, **not** the other way around. From a slightly different angle, how they are choosing to milk their passion drives their selection of success criteria.

This might seem incidental , but it is a critical point to understand. You probably started out your career (and life to varying degrees) by looking at how you could satiate socially or family-accepted success metrics—income levels, title, big corner office, and so on—with relatively little thought or even care as to the journey as long as it maximized the possibility of attaining them. Looking back, at least in my case, this was due to a combination of ignorance of the sheer number of journeys that exist, laziness or fear for not wanting to explore them, and an unhealthy attachment to my work. The really nasty part about these factors is that they can easily collude, creating a "No Exit" kind of scenario.

Have you ever felt like wherever you work would crumble if you left? Have you ever felt such a strong commitment to your customers or work colleagues that you postponed looking for something else for fear of leaving them to be handled by someone less qualified? I suffered this malaise for three years in my first job out of college. Although my employer did need to hire three people to take my place when I finally left, lo and behold, the world kept spinning, gravity was still in effect, and the sun still rose in the East. What a mistake I had made, watching three years of my life fritter away into semiparanoid deliria. (I actually developed Chronic Fatigue Syndrome, which my research reveals is more psychological than physical in nature.) Although I was passionate about my work, I didn't have the experience, wherewithal, or confidence to think I could focus it elsewhere or that my skill sets could have value in a different context.

The journey drives your metrics. If you are Virginia, you shouldn't expect to make a million dollars or be seen on *Oprah*, at least for your first couple of years out. But Virginia can throw clay every day, and she is happily succeeding on her terms. Eddie might not be able to bring in a million dollars in training revenues or get his picture on the cover of *Business Week* or even *Bicycling* any time soon, but he can happily ride every day, and he is succeeding on his terms with a smile the size of a bike wheel spinning on his face. Jules might never grow large enough to gross a million smackers per year or be able to afford her own art collector. However, she has been able to throw the fictitious art/life balance into Virginia's kiln, and she is succeeding, on her terms.

This is a critical point to contemplate. Again, your journey defines how you define your measures of success, not the other way around. It doesn't matter if you are a politician, salesperson, schoolteacher, tech support rep, marketing maven, nurse, or union negotiator. Your chosen path is intertwined with your definitions of success in life, be they rising in influence in different levels of government, enlightening customers as to the benefit of your wares, helping 3,000 kids over the course of your career understand and delight in American history, assisting your daily quota plus 20 percent in making their computers productive again, increasing your market share by 5 percent, helping 10,000 patients get better, or putting airlines out of business. Understanding your personal success metrics while staying true to your other priorities, whatever they might be, properly aligns your mission with how you spell "success."

Success Is in the Eye of the Beholder or the Beholden?

I have asked many people from all walks of life how they define success. Here are some of my favorite answers:

- "Success is not having to worry about things."
- "Success is having the time to do what you want to do."

- "Success is giving your kids the confidence and esteem to allow them to do whatever they want to do."
- "Success is figuring out what is most important to you and then sticking to it."
- "Success is being able to travel wherever and whenever I want."
- "Success is being able to retire early."
- "Success is loving my job."
- "Success is not wanting anything."

Obviously, the way you define success depends completely on you—who you are, what is important to you, what you want out of your LifeTime, and so on. What is interesting about these responses is that money was not blatantly mentioned—no dollar amounts, houses on the hill, or yachts in the harbor. Yes, you need money to travel, and retiring early implies having some dough in the bank, although the number of zeros required to meet either definition is open to a wide range of requirements. Fundamentally, you define your metrics for success.

Or do you? I just received an e-mail from a good friend looking for people to audition for the next series of *The Apprentice*, the reality TV show in which Donald Trump, hard-charging business icon, interviews candidates to head up one of his divisions with a salary upward of $200,000 plus perks, options, yadda. The criteria read as follows,

> *Young, attractive, successful, smart, and obviously able to leave their present situation for 3 weeks.*

What does "successful" mean in this context? Do you see any blatant overlaps with the previously mentioned interpretations? You probably don't see anything you would want to bet on. No, in this context, "successful" means having money—lots of money. It means having the ability to prance into Trump Tower, cameras rolling and lights glaring, sporting the latest Brooks Brothers' or Burberry suit. It means being able to throw down your Gucci bag or wallet, kick up your Luis Vitton or Bruno Maglia loafers, and glance at your Rolex to give The Don a hard time if he is late.

The reason I picked this slightly cheesy example is that *The Apprentice* is a condensed version of elemental aspects of our society that you might both love and hate. Greed is glorified, hardnosed testosterone rules, ethics and teams are chucked out the window, and please pity the poor bastard or bastardette who just doesn't have what it takes to work for Mr. Trump. Don't get me wrong here; I am quite certain you love the thrill and power of competition, as long as you are competing for something you actually want. Given *The Apprentice*'s ratings, though, it seems you love to compete merely for the goal, journey be damned.

This duality of both admiring and despising these crass and barbaric elements of our mores vividly mirrors your internal wearing and tearing in how you define success. Capitalism is anchored on competition, and our entire socioeconomic structure, from top to bottom, has been built to reward those who can perform. And there is nothing wrong with this. The difficulty arises when you confuse financial success with your own personal versions. It is hard—in fact, impossible—to escape the blur. You could be in the wilds of Wyoming, neck deep in Northern Vermont snow, or on an Arizona Indian reservation, accessible only by mule train or helicopter. All you need is a mailing address, and Pottery-Sonoma-Olily Never-Never Land can be delivered to your cabin step.

An interesting parallel can be made by looking at what separates the abilities of professional athletes. Success to an athlete is simple: winning. It's not placing second or third, but winning—being number 1, world champion, best in class—that is the sole goal. At a certain level, per my readings and forays into this arena, there comes a point, past training, conditioning, and computer analysis of your stroke-stride-tuck-turn-swing-push, where your success is determined not by competing with others but by competing with yourself, or -selves in a team context. It becomes about competing for confidence, for focus, for believing you can win. The host of external variables—"She is taller than me," "He beat me the last time," "They have a great reputation for defense," "Their budget is so much larger than ours"—becomes dramatically less important as the race-round-game draws to a close.

There are countless examples of this inward versus outward focus being the key differentiator between "the triumph of high achievement and the agony of defeat," as *ABC Wide World of Sports* used to lead off its segments. Think of the Japanese Olympic speed skater in Nagano, handicapped with relatively shorter legs, who won the Gold out of sheer force of will. Or consider the story behind the film *Hoosiers*, where height, experience, and budget appeared to be considerable factors. If you haven't seen this classic in a while, I strongly suggest giving it a whirl or download. Even the Boston Red Sox's miraculous triumph over the New York Yankees and then progressively blowing the St. Louis Cardinals out of their cage in the 2004 World Series was enabled by this dynamic.

The parallel between *The Apprentice* and professional sports is this: All things considered and everything tallied, you must individually define your version of success, which ain't easy. Our social underpinnings have been poured in a concrete mold that defines success as beating others and basking in the financial reward of that victory, be it on the playing field or in the boardroom. Chipping away at this mammoth foundation with a mere crowbar emblazoned with "How Do I Define Success" is a difficult task, but it's one your core can readily handle. Like most journeys, the trick is making that first monumentally small yet requisite step.

So what is success? Success is simply doing what you want to do; what you were born to do; what your passions keep reminding you that you should be doing. Success is defining your journey—living on your terms—because this control fundamentally provides happiness. Unfortunately, living this simple corollary might be a quantum leap. You probably weren't raised, educated, or socially conditioned to understand and abide by this principle. You might have been so hung up on getting into the best school possible, on landing the "best" job possible, on living in the trendiest location possible that you have forgotten what your greatest possible possibilities are. It's not that these milestones aren't noble or valid, as long as they don't obscure or cloud your understandings of success. Look at them as *outcomes* of your journey or dividends of your investments, rather than mere *objectives*. You have been scared into believing that "safer" routes are better, that degrees enable happiness, that committing yourself to something you don't particularly like but earns a ton of dough in 10 or 15 years makes you better than everyone else when, from my humble perspective, it must be one of the saddest situations I can think of. Talk about accelerating your personal depreciation. You aren't a cat.

WHAT IS THE END GAME?

Or perhaps more appropriately, what is **your** end game? Deep down inside, don't you simply want to be happy? Happy with yourself, happy with where you are in life, happy with your work, and happy with future prospects? This was the second pattern from the preceding stories: All three are visibly happy, and this contentment has spilled all over their LifeTimes! Attaining and maintaining a certain level of happiness might be the best definition of "success" you could ever hope to realize. **Do you want to die unhappy?** What a waste that would be! You have studied and worked so hard and so long, you have done everything you are supposed to do, yet at the end of your days, you aren't happy... and then you die. Yes, there will be points and even stretches in your LifeTime where you will be distraught, frustrated, and downright bummed. This is unavoidable. Inevitably, however, with your core at your side, you control your incredibly resilient state of mind. I defy the "safety in the middle" theory that people describe as their means of "monitoring" their happiness. The concept basically avoids experiencing extreme levels of happiness because in so doing you expose yourself to similar ranges on the downside. Not only is this categorically **wimpy**, but it is patently faulty. Swings (like X-Factors) *will happen*, and you must be ready to deal with both limits. Simultaneously, though, you are the master and commander of your personal vessel. *You* decide if you want it to sink or float.

Why is being happy so important? I'd like to introduce the first of a couple of references to an extraordinary report issued on June 17, 2004 by James Montier of the London Global Equities Strategy group of the German investment bank, Dresdner Kleinwort Wasserstein. These reports typically provide overviews and updates as to how world events might impact market and company performances. The name of the report is "If It Makes You Happy," and it explores the psychology of happiness. In typical English humor, this report starts off quoting that famous Monty Python line, "And now, for something completely different...." (And yes, this *is* different.) His research of psychological literature reveals some mind-shattering benefits of being happy, which he has consolidated into three categories:

- **Social rewards**—Higher odds of marriage and lower odds of divorce, more friends, stronger social support, and richer social interactions.

- **Superior work outcomes**—Greater creativity, increased productivity, higher quality of work, higher income, and more activity and energy
- **Personal benefits**—Bolstered immune system, greater longevity, and greater self control and coping abilities

Interestingly, these benefits intuitively mirror those generated by working your passions. Montier then presents his top ten suggestions for improving your happiness. There are some golden nuggets sparkling in your face here.

1. Don't equate happiness with money. You can adapt to income shifts relatively quickly. The long-lasting effects are basically zero.

2. Exercise regularly. Taking regular exercise generates further energy and stimulates your mind and body.

3. Have sex (preferably with someone you love). Sex is consistently rated as among the highest generators of happiness. So what are you waiting for?

4. Devote time and effort to close relationships. Close relationships require work and effort but pay vast rewards in terms of happiness.

5. Pause for reflection, and meditate on the good things in life. Simple reflection on the good aspects of life helps prevent "hedonic adaptation" (to be defined in a bit).

6. Seek work that engages your skills, and look to enjoy your job. It makes sense to do something you enjoy. This is turn is likely to allow you to flourish at your job, creating a pleasant feedback loop.

7. Give your body the sleep it needs.

8. Don't pursue happiness for its own sake. Enjoy the moment. Faulty perceptions of what makes you

happy might lead to the wrong pursuits. Additionally, activities might become a means to an end, rather than something to be enjoyed, defeating the purpose in the first place.

9. Take control of your life, and set achievable goals.
10. Remember to follow all the rules. (This comes from England, after all.)

I couldn't agree more with all of them (even number 10, which my internal compass magnetically tries to avoid). Numbers 6—looking to enjoy your job—and 9—control through achievable goals—should hopefully ring with magnified resonance.

Allow me to share a story about a man whose mere presence personified these commandments and provided some much-needed perspective. I don't know his name, and we only met in passing, but his smile, demeanor, stride, and the gleam in his eyes were among the happiest I have ever witnessed. I was on the north shore of Bali, at a little thatched hut enclave called Lovina Beach, ephemerally seeking refuge from a corporate Inferno into which I had knowingly descended. The sun was setting, and I was out on the beach, soaking up the colors of its glorious, waning arc.

A local fisherman, wearing only tattered shorts and a floppy sun hat, casually sauntered by carrying a bamboo pole over one shoulder, his daily catch dangling off the long end. At this point in time, the average Indonesian brought in $220 *per year* (60 cents per day). He was whistling a carefree tune, and his barefoot gait echoed his melody. He saw me, immediately smiled, nodded his head, and then beamed again. He and his family were going to eat well that night! I will never forget thinking to myself, "He has no 401(k) or IRA. He has no mortgage or car, probably doesn't know the word for portfolio in his language, and odds are he probably doesn't even have a bank account. Nor does he need one. Yet he is so much more visibly stoked than I am with his netted bag of fish. What the hell is wrong with me?"

I wonder if those victorious *Apprentice* contestants will ever be as happy as this fisherman.

KISS (KEEP IT SIMPLE, STUPID)

Our developed-country clutter you find yourself trying to sort through (and you need to, no doubt) underscores a need to keep things as simple as possible. KISS. Ever hear this slightly conde-scending expression at work? I certainly have. "Kang, this PowerPoint slide is brilliant! You have captured all five dimensions of our client's strategic and operational issues in the confines of our three-dimensional time/space continuum. The ultraviolet glasses we need to wear to view this model are a bit clumsy, and the bat-tery life could be better, but they work. One minor question, though: What do all these animated lines, bullet-pointed gobbly-gook, and filled-in circles mean?"

I believe you want as simple a life as possible. Why would you want an overtly complex life? Why might you dream of owning a winery or olive farm in Northern California, Tuscany, or the South of France? Because the lifestyle harkens back to a time before Reality TV, before the need to schedule "time to reflect," a time when the word *wireless* referred to a grapevine that managed to lose its stake. A funny thing about our mass-marketed technology-laden society is that most things you buy, from shaving supplies to car rentals, have been designed to simplify your life. Some do. Many don't. Look at your computer desktop. How many "short-cut" icons have magically appeared over time, taking up space and making the process of finding things that much more difficult? A question from a different realm: Why does the average American kitchen require 35 cubic feet of storage space? It's to cache all those nifty contraptions you rarely use that have been designed to make your life easier. What do you need to do to access this 35 cubic feet, costing on average upward of $5,000 in most metropolitan environments? Build a bigger kitchen, of course. Even better, buy a bigger house! The price of simplicity.

A secret to keeping life simple and happy is simply not wanting. This is a very Zen concept. It is in the act of desiring something that unhappiness is born; the pretense of gaining happiness through a tangible object is immature at a basic level. "Well, frankly, I don't have the time to be enlightened. I'd rather keep my hair, and the last time I was able to sit cross-legged for more than two minutes without keeling over in extreme pain was around the campfire at Camp Whatchamacallit when I was 11," you might be thinking to yourself. Or something along these lines.

What the Zen folks are implicitly saying here is that our personal happiness cannot be driven by material objects. Think about it for a moment. Do you really think anything you could ever buy would bring you sheer, unadulterated, and sustainable happiness? Other than a Diaper Genie and wireless router, I can't think of **anything** imparting such an ongoing level of satisfaction and joy. Seriously, happiness comes from within. Being happy is a state of mind, which you can control, certain chemical imbalances notwithstanding. I'd like to share two recent studies that support this millennia-old Zen concept that material goods, and implicitly the money needed to buy them, do not provide happiness, but love and relationships do.

One study conducted by the University of Southern California tracked more than 1,500 people for nearly 30 years and revealed that there was no correlation between increases in income and increases in happiness. In fact, people who made more money and could buy more things tended to get caught up in self-destructive, neverending loops of acquisition, an addiction to consumption that could never be satiated. The study's findings concluded that happiness is driven by your ability to spend time with those you love and your health.

A second study, which surveyed 7,167 students in 41 countries of dramatically different standards of living, drew a similar conclusion. Those respondents who valued love more than money reported far higher life satisfaction than those who appeared to be focused on financial gain.

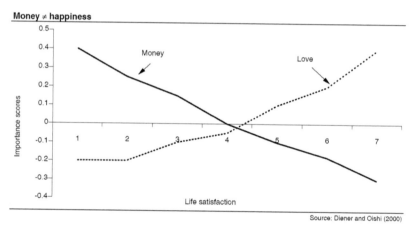

Money ≠ happiness

Source: Diener and Oishi (2000)

FIGURE 3.1   Graph of money versus love.

THE RULE OF 85 PERCENT

I'd like to refer back to the Stockdale Paradox to set a vitally important and baseline expectation. The expectation is this: You can make tremendous improvements to the time of your life; however, the cold hard facts dictate that **you will never be completely, eternally happy**. Yes, you might experience brief and possibly prolonged interludes of bliss, hopefully emanating from a raised level of baseline happiness. Whatever you want to call it, though—Nirvana, Enlightenment, Equilibrium, or perhaps more appropriately, the life depicted in *Martha Stewart* or *Men's Health* magazines—simply doesn't exist in this world. These depictions might serve as tempting escapes to ponder and purchase, but at the end of the day, they are delusions. It doesn't matter if you religiously follow the upcoming process of the Five Ps and realize and actualize your mission. Until the day you die, there will always be burrs in your worry socks and snags in your happy sweaters within and without your control. That's just the way you are. You exist; thus, problems of some degree must exist, too.

This said, I must reiterate my belief that you can experience incremental and even dramatic increases in your happy factors. The **real** question is about your expectations of what you are looking for. A recent dinner at a friend's house yielded an insightful metric I'd like to share with you in this context. My friends called it the rule of 85 percent. The more I reflected on it, the more I liked it. Basically, if 85 percent of whatever they were looking for was there, they agreed they would be happy with it. Looking at a new house, new car, new camera, school for the kids, work, whatever— if it had 85 percent of the functions and features, it was a done deal. If it didn't, they would keep looking. I see this as an expectation grounded in reality. Is it possible to get everything you want, all the time? Absolutely not. Is it possible to get close? Most certainly yes. Should you try to get close? Without a doubt! But before you kill yourself trying to find that perfect shingle house with the extra bedroom, built-ins, separated home office, kitchen counters made to the statistical average of your close family's height in a quiet cul de sac, a three-minute walk from the train and organic grocery, you must accept that **nothing** is perfect. Call it compromising all you want, but the rule of 85 percent is a rational and realistic way of working through a prioritized group of expectations.

Although the concepts, stories, and tools presented in this book are intended to significantly reduce the size, pain, and frequency of your issues, you cannot regard them as magical panaceas that can cure, purge, or protect you from the raw good and bad facts of existence. In truth of fact, I don't think you would like such a shell either because the implicit claustrophobia would probably drive you batty. I would like to protect you with the best suit of armor possible, though, which means going another level deeper into understanding the roots of happiness. Understanding enables control. This naturally means giving your stodgy investment banker at Dresdner Kleinwort Wasserstein another ring.

THE ROOTS OF HAPPINESS

I'd like to again refer to Montier's report. Per his research, there are three fundamental roots of your happiness. The first is your genetic makeup, which contributes 50 percent of your overall happy quotient. Although tremendous advances are being made in understanding and altering both your neurochemical reactions and actual genetic composition, it will be a few years before any "unhappy sequences" can be safely removed or rehabilitated. Merely feigning knowledge of this driver is way out of my league, and I encourage you to research this topic more if you'd like. The other half of this equation consists of two categories: life circumstances and intentional activity.

Life circumstances, which include virtually every aspect of your existence from marital status, financial security, geographic setting, religious affiliation, and so on surprisingly account for **only 10 percent** of the variations in your happiness. These factors tend to transition relatively quickly and suffer the ignominy of the brutal term "hedonic adaptation," the notion that gains in particular forms of happiness quickly become the norm. Moving to California might cause an initial increase in happiness; however, that level will over time become part of your baseline happy standard. This dynamic can be seen in the fact that the percentage of Americans who describe themselves as "very happy" has remained disturbingly constant, ranging between roughly 27 to 38 percent over the past 50 years and narrowing from 29 to 34 percent over the past 30, a period of time during which Americans recorded tremendous increases in income per capita. Clearly, hedonic adaptation (our standard of living to various degrees) is alive and thriving and, for its relative contribution to your happiness, would seem to take up an inordinate amount of LifeTime.

The third factor, which represents a whopping 40 percent of your happiness and is intuitively where you should focus the majority of your efforts, are intentional activities, or "discrete actions or activities" you can choose to do. These actions can be segmented into three categories:

- **Behavioral activities**—Regular exercise, more-than-regular sex, socializing, and so on.
- **Cognitive activities**—Trying to see the glass as half full (and imagining it getting fuller), taking the time to review how fortunate you are, and so on.
- **Volitional activities**—The process of resolutely trying to meet your personal goals, dedicating energy to meaningful causes, and so on.

How you behave (or don't) is completely up to you, and this work cannot directly influence the number of daily sit-ups or yoga positions you might be trying to complete. Yes, it can have an indirect effect, through outputs from the Five Ps, but these selections are by your volition. Similarly, I'm pretty certain that the last thing

you want is someone else controlling your perspective and reminding you in a helium-induced voice just how lucky you are while
stuck in a traffic logjam.

Enabling your volitional activities, as defined earlier, is the best
use of this book going forward, starting with the big one, per
Rockefeller: How do you want to "efficiently and satisfyingly use
the great wealth" you have been born into? How can you find and
benefit from those "meaningful causes" that will facilitate your
ongoing happiness? Let me be extremely clear here. "Meaningful"
does **not** necessarily imply causes of a nonprofit or governmental
nature. As the Five Ps will illustrate, the respective meaning of
your causes is completely up to you. It is motivated by your mission and depends on whatever proficiencies and priorities you are
dealing with. Yes, a large degree of the Five Ps' outputs will focus
on changing or adapting your working life to new and groovier scenarios. This said, it is the process of actualizing these changes that
generates significantly more and lasting happiness. This might
explain why that Nike slogan "Just Do It" has blown doors for
more than a decade.

A recent study supports this hypothesis that it is the practice
of personal achievement that breeds ongoing and sustainable happiness. Scientists at Emory University monitored neural activity in
the region of our brains where pleasure and reward register. Two
groups of people played a computer game. One was required to
successfully complete a set of arduous tasks before receiving a
prize, whereas the other scored regardless of how they fared.
When the prize arrived, only those who had earned it recorded
significant activity in this key part of the brain. "From the brain's
perspective, earning it is more meaningful and probably more satisfying," observes researcher Gregory Berns. "I don't think [the
brain] ever evolved to sit back and sit on the couch and have things
fall in our lap." This could explain the higher than normal suicide

rate in those "lucky" lottery winners. Simply stated, you are hard-wired to want to succeed because it is this process of achievement that makes you happy.

The best part about this dynamic is that it will never end. Just when you think you have this life thing under your thumb, some random X-Factor, an emerging priority, or a different expression of your mission will either knock softly or break down your door. ("Mr. Gorbachev, tear down this wall!") The opportunities to initiate or restart volitional activities will never go away, implicitly providing a LifeTime of potential happiness.

You might be saying to yourself, "Why is all this ongoing improvement necessarily such a *good* thing? I mean, I just want to be able to fish all day." Simple. One of the worst conditions you could ever hope to have (aside from ALS) is boredom. The first stop to hell on earth is boredom, or to quote Voltaire in *Candide*, "It is through work that we find happiness. Boredom leads to Sin." Being distracted for a little while is completely cool and probably a good thing. Spending time doing nothing at all is also a noteworthy idea. But being bored and doing nothing about it is an irreplaceable waste of LifeTime.

"Okay. I promise to work on behaving myself and thinking a bit more. I can handle those activities. How do I start this volitional process? Where do I start? What do I need to start? What is the magic bullet that will bring down the specter of whatever is holding me back?"

CHAPTER 4

THE MAGIC BULLET

Passion. Merely saying the word—how the consonants and vowels start emanating from your lips as they pucker and then end with a relaxed and sensual hush—evokes a myriad of powerful images, sensations, and emotions that link to a primeval and unquenchable energy within. Passion. A force so strong that, unbridled, it is dangerous. Recently, you might have noticed more uses of the word in advertising and corporate identity campaigns. "Your possibilities. Our passion." Microsoft touts visually and verbally. "Refined with a passion," extols Lexus in its Web and TV expressions. You might also hear about CEOs and others with Big Wigs extolling the virtues of working your passions.

"Okay, hold on now," you say to yourself. "Something here is fishy. In my mind, passion and work simply don't mix. Yes, there are things I love to do, but I don't think anyone in his right mind would ever dream of paying me to do them. I don't care who says so—a job is a job." Allow this slightly cracked head to attempt to let a little light through.

PEOPLE SHOULD PAY YOU TO WORK YOUR PASSIONS

Huh? Why should anyone pay me to do what I love to do? The answer glares, yet it is seemingly ignored in your quest for fitting job descriptions, scaling the title wall, and getting the best possible name on your résumé, which I understand, along with your credit rating, is standard criteria when you meet St. Peter at the pearly gates. Why? Imagine actually looking forward to getting to work. Imagine, other priorities being satiated, not caring if you spend until 11 at night working on a proposal. Imagine your personal productivity increasing by a log and the consequent opportunities that will come knocking at your door or on your phone from recruiters. Imagine managing a team of impassioned colleagues and the impact this would have on **both** your and their performance reviews. Imagine the impact that drawing on passions would have on a business unit, or hell, an entire company's earnings per share numbers. Are you hallucinating here? Simply put, working your passions can transform a mere job into your life's work.

Not only **should** people pay you to work your passion, they **will** pay you (quite nicely) to work them. There are some designations here that are important to zero in on aside from the obvious "What is my passion?", which will be smothered in the Five Ps. The key question is who are these people who will be paying you? It could be a government body at some level. It could be a nonprofit focused on a particular issue. It could be a grungy start-up to a corporate goliath. They could be donors to **your** nonprofit organization. They could be consumers, businesses, or retailers gobbling up your wares. They could be businesses who need your services. What is critical to understand is that as long as you can define your passion, **someone** will pay you to live on your terms. You might not make millions, but intuitively, you have a much greater chance of this outcome if you do.

A NOTE FROM THE BOSS

A couple years ago, I had the distinct pleasure to listen to a speech delivered by one of the most reputable CEOs in American corporate history. I can still recite one line he said more or less verbatim, "Whatever you do, be yourself and work with passion." This particular CEO was able to grow his company's value by $500 **billion** in 20 years with an average return on equity exceeding 20%. Any ideas whom this might have been? It was none other than Jack Welch, former CEO of General Electric.

This quote to work with passion struck me as a bit funny coming from the CEO of one of the largest and most powerful corporations in the world. Be yourself? Work with passion? For decades, I had the distinct impression that GE was the kind of place where everyone wore blue suits, shaved using Mach 3 or Venus razors twice daily, and started work with a rousing chorus of "We Bring Good Things to Life" in various languages around the world. Here is the leader extolling individuality and emotion as the key drivers of his employee's success. The guy has more money, fame, and corporate clout than you might want to imagine, yet it is exhibiting what drives you that drives his respect.

I had to read his book *Jack*, which clearly confirmed one basic principle that supports the point that people will pay you to work your passion: The best way to attract, retain, grow, and promote people, which is **the** key to organizational growth, is by aligning their passions with the corporate mission. Mr. Welch clearly understood this. This factor, more than any other, is what he attributed GE's continued stellar results.

ANOTHER DATA POINT

I'd like to introduce another quote along this line. "Working your passion increases the odds of your success—**however you define it**—to 90%." This statement came from an interview with Erin Moore, a 20-year human resources veteran in DuPont, who left as vice president of the Medical Systems Group. She continued, "I have seen all sorts of management fads, business models, and organization structures come and go... **By far**, the most important factor in any organization's success is its ability to draw on its employees' passions." I am not necessarily a betting man, but if the odds were a 90% win, I'd plunk down my kids' 529 plans in a heartbeat.

No better example, she professed, was the case of her Medical Systems Group. It produced and serviced nuclear resonance technology, whose functionality had long been outdated and outshined by the ongoing march of technical progress. Even with such a difficult situation, the Group was still able to grow results in excess of 20% per year. How? "The group's management was passionate about their technology and firmly believed it still had a place in the market. This passion attracted employees of a similar nature, and the rest resides in our results."

I also like this quote because Ms. Moore sagaciously frames success in holistic parameters—"however you define it." I am going to make a sexist statement here, so please bear with me. Women typically (and thankfully) define success differently than men. Yes, we share similar concepts; however, women typically rank certain factors—that is, lifestyle and raising kids—higher than men. Women innately understand that there is more to life than merely making the most money and attaining the uber-title. Testosterone verses estrogen? Perhaps. Regardless, Ms. Moore's caveat directly supports the "Whatever you do (in life), do it with

Passion" maxim introduced a couple of chapters back. If you want to succeed in life, what better way to do it than tapping and releasing your passion in every facet of your existence?

Reflect for a moment on how many different channels exist outside of your working life to release your passions. What you do in your spare time? What are your hobbies, sports, organizations or clubs, and volunteer activities? Who is your peer group, or more specifically, the kind of people you like to interact with? If you have kids, look at how you are raising them and the directions in which you are perhaps unconsciously guiding them. Heck, take a gander at the demographics of the community where you live, the kind of structure you live in, and the art on your walls. All of these facets of life serve as visible releases of your passions.

THE PASSION PRINCIPLE

There is presently and unfortunately a void of credible data linking job satisfaction and income potential. I'm sure you've heard the phrase, "Do what you love, and the money will follow." It sounds nifty and enticing, but for those of us who only desire and can handle the truth, a scientific study reinforcing or disproving this aphorism would be welcomed. If you know of such a study or would like to initiate one, please let me know. Intuitively and anecdotally though, this advice, what I call the Passion Principle, seems to ring true. More importantly, from my humble perspective, if you love what you are doing, if you are passionate about your work, life will follow in a multitude of shimmering manifestations—richer relationships, less stress, overall happiness, and so on. I'd like to share three illustrations of the power of this principle at play.

The first exceptional example of someone who profited from her passions is the story of Julie Aigner-Clark, founder of the Baby

Einstein Company. Her passion is instilling a love of art and literature, both of which she taught, into kids. She was a new mother
and realized there was a glaring need for stimulating videos for
infants—not cartoons or games, but videos that would promote a
love of humanities and art in kids. In 1997, she plunked $15,000
into creating a homemade video, shot in her basement and edited
on a Macintosh computer. She then talked a retailer into introducing it in six of its stores. First-year sales approached $100,000. But
that was just the tip of the iceberg.

Ms. Aigner-Clark's second video, *Baby Mozart*, came to market with the release of a UC Berkeley study linking increased
childhood mental development with classical music. (Sadly, the
definition of "classical" is not the same as some local radio stations
that include the likes of Led Zeppelin and now even Devo in their
"classic" play lists.) From there on, Baby Einstein started pushing
the space-time continuum in terms of relative speed of growth.
Seven years later, Baby Einstein's projected revenues for 2004
were $100 million+!

Most importantly, Ms. Aigner-Clark realized when to get out.
Five years into growing the company, she found herself struggling
to meet the demands of her professional and Mommy responsibilities, so she sold her company to The Walt Disney Company,
although she is still involved as a creative consultant. The following quote sums up Ms. Aigner-Clark to a tee: "Be passionate
about your ideas, and never forget what's important in life. I attrib-
ute Baby Einstein's success to my passion for the subjects featured
in the videos and books."

Here's another story about a similar passion-principled success. In 1977, three young men born of the 1960s counterculture
were looking for a way to remain true to their "irresponsible" roots.
They came up with a book called *Juggling for the Complete Klutz*,
which included three beanbags in its fishnet packaging. Soon they

realized they were on to something breathtakingly novel—actually including devices with the instructions. Yoyos, hackey sacks, and other things followed, and their product and title lines expanded to more than 150 different offerings. In 2000, the three sold the company named Klutz to Scholastic for $73 million. One of the founders, John Cassidy, now serves as creative lead. He summed up my version of the passion principle (…Life will follow) nicely, "A personal note to those who run their own businesses: If you only reap one reward—the one that goes to the bank—you're underpaid." They get it—without an MBA!

The last example comes from someone whom Jack Welch most certainly respects. He is a relatively successful investor who, during a meeting with some University of Tennessee business school students, responded to the question of how to pick the right first job out of school with the following observations:

> *"Never do what you don't enjoy.*
> *Doing so is like saving sex for old age.*
> *Not a very good idea."*

Any guesses who this investor (worth in the neighborhood of $46 billion, give or take a couple hundred million) might be? It's Warren Buffet, the Oracle of Omaha. Even with the introduction of Viagra and other such enhancers, I posit Buffet would still deem this practice as not being the best of life plans.

BUSINESS SCHOOL RECRUITING, METAPHORICALLY SPEAKING

Here is a fascinating statistic that might be applicable to many of you who have attended or recruited us smarty-pants MBAs. For a while now, roughly 75% of Wharton and Harvard Business School graduates have changed employers if not industries within

two years of graduation, the Harvard grads making the switch on average only 18 months into their hard-fought and negotiated placements. Thinking back to how much time and money corporate recruiters spent attracting candidates to their presentations and wining and dining at "sell" events, I have to wonder what their desired hurdle rate of extracted value from these unequivocally brilliant but still fresh recruits might be.

This factoid reflects three overwhelming factors that you must confront as your career unfolds, the business school recruiting process being a giga-hyped version of these issues. First, of course, is the money factor. How much money can I make? How big was your signing bonus (again)? What is the total package worth to me NOW, given certain equations and drivers holding constant? We have an unfortunate natural tendency to equate any kind of performance, particularly those that can be defined in numerical terms, with success and even worse, the "I'm better than you syndrome." Because there is sadly no universally recognized, FDA-approved Happy Meter at your disposal, the money factor quickly takes the de facto leading position as judge **and** jury.

Number crunchers were finally given their chance to shine as they garnered their analyst offers. Other bold pioneers accepted their offers early, establishing benchmarks that simply had to be bested. Returning to the previous tenure results, though, the money factor apparently wasn't enough to keep graduates happy. In fact, it might have become more of a hindrance than a help because taking a pay cut to make a move is the last thing anyone in his wrong mind would want to do. Let me be clear here: If you find your dream opportunity, by all means try to get the best deal possible, but don't waste your LifeTime going after opportunities solely or even primarily because of the money factor.

The Magic Bullet

Second is the utterly powerful sex appeal of working for the elite firms in whatever ecosystem of the world you operate. There will always be those organizations you regard as The Best, and this can be a good goal, passion permitting. The cachet, branded reputation, and networks afforded by gaining employment by the leading company in your desired industry can quickly springboard you to new plateaus. The downside to this quest is that the "what" of what you are doing can too easily be overshadowed and lost by details of the "who" you will be potentially working for.

As an example, I heard and can well imagine (but could not confirm) that upward of 65% of a recent Harvard Business School class applied to work at the Grand PooBah of consulting firms, McKinsey & Company. Although most of the applicants might have been qualified for the experience, I can guarantee nowhere near that percentage of applicants would be able to focus their passion on the kind of work and particular culture intrinsic to McKinsey. Let me be clear here: Consulting, like **all** other industries, offers the opportunity to release your passions in uniquely novel ways. From experience, though, only a small percentage of the population has been built and prioritized to be happy focusing the excessive amount of LifeTime that this profession demands.

A contributing factor to this appeal is the prolific herd mentality toward certain industries. I will never forget watching the fodder sway with each new sector that made its debut. First came the investment banks. For a solid three weeks, everyone was trying to figure out how to "de-lever Beta." Then came the consulting shops, and for another three weeks, "value creation" and dismembering the most treacherous case studies were the hot topics. After that was consumer products and next technology. Of course, business school students being what they are, who would ever think of considering a firm that didn't come to campus?

This dynamic, combined with the money factor, can produce unfortunate stories like the following.

An exceedingly smart and charismatic Wharton candidate had his pick of industries and firms. He quickly garnered offers from the top investment banks and consulting firms, and after some negotiations, he chose to join one of the latter. He spent his signing bonus traveling the world the summer after graduation and eagerly looked forward to starting in the fall. The middle of his first week on the job, he realized he had made a serious mistake. He realized that consulting, the firm, or some combination of the two wasn't right for him. What should he do? All his other offers had been withdrawn, those positions filled, and if he didn't stay a certain period of time, he would owe the firm a fairly hefty chunk of change. To his credit, though, he realized he had made a mistake early on and was able to reload his LifeTime 24 months sooner than the majority of his classmates. 24 months might not seem like a lot, but a hell of a lot of X-Factors can happen in two years, or even two heartbeats. Net sum: Be sure your passions fit the employer for whom you want to work.

The third and by far most endemic and daunting factor is simply this:

You don't know what you don't know.

Do you have **any** idea what other job opportunities exist for someone with your skill sets and life experiences? Do you know distinctly what your skill sets are? What you excel at, and what you could improve? Do you know what you love to do, **aside** from what you might good at? To what extent does the context of your work—your function, your company, your industry, or your boss's management style—influence what you think you excel at and love to do? How might the unique combination of your personality, values, and personal experiences be levered in other contexts? Aside from the standard Meyers-Briggs test I took at Wharton, which most memorably accurately reflected the fact that I like to surf, none of the questions I mention were even glossed over during my stay. Have you ever been asked these questions? Odds are you haven't, but if you have, you are a couple large steps ahead of my Wharton class in terms of figuring out how to live in the time of your life.

The amount of ignorance of these arguably important details was matched by a lack of information regarding similarly significant aspects of potential employers. Yes, I knew that investment bankers made a lot of money, worked sick hours, and lived for their bonuses. Consultants got paid well and traveled incessantly, saving companies from the brink of extinction. But this was about all I knew or cared to know. Aside from starting a company, the saintly nobility of becoming a corporate Lazarus was compelling enough, the money was good, so pass on everything else. Laziness combined with not wanting or having a process to understand yourself will never lead to anything extraordinary. As Thomas Edison insightfully observed, "Everything comes to those that hustle while they wait." Look where laziness led in this case... **1,200 years** of LifeTime **per class**, not wasted but similarly not optimized.

It requires work, dedication, commitment, perseverance, maybe some sacrifice, and a fair chunk of LifeTime to unearth both the internal and external factors that need to combine for you to hit your sweet spot. The question simply becomes this: How much more of your LifeTime do you want to spend before you do?

SOME PRELIMINARY DATA

There is a fascinating aspect to the back end of this hiring process that deserves some attention. In the first of hopefully many such studies, a Harvard Business School Doctoral Candidate and business school friend, Connie Hadley, explored subjective and objective factors explaining why 600+ business school graduates "loved their jobs." (Incidentally, only 22% of respondents reported "loving their jobs.") The really fascinating aspect of her initial results (further studies need to be done with larger groups) is that there was **no** correlation among those who loved their jobs and the amount of money they were bringing in. It didn't matter if they used their degrees for social work and brought in 50k or really cashed in and brought in 500k—the amount of money they earned did not influence their love for their jobs in the slightest.

BRINGING IT HOME

By now, you are probably sick of reading about those pampered business school kids and all their melodramatic trials and tribulations in finding employment. I mean sheesh, don't they have every major corporation on the planet banging down their doors? There is a reason why they have been receiving my focus. Simply put: They are just like the rest of us, only they have been able to secure low-interest debt to give them two years to conceptually focus on where they see themselves five years from now, all X-Factors and ignorance aside. In this context, I might argue they are actually more risk averse than the average citizen. Why else would one forfeit two years and a ton of interest? Yes, they are competitive, but then again, aren't you also competitive when something you really want is at stake (or perhaps equally as relevant, when you are scared of "failure")? The friendships, networks, and branding that an MBA bestows are incredibly valuable, no question about it, and the education and corporate contacts can be useful. These factors aside, an MBA merely **accelerates** your rate of promotion and potential earning power, which is NOT to say you couldn't rise to whatever position you desired, if your passions are aligned, you're focused, and you're patient.

PASSIONATE MONSTERS

I recently did a search of all the résumés posted on Monster.com in a six-month period. Although I wasn't able to verify the exact number of resumes I was searching, if you consider that Monster welcomes 1.6 million visitors per day looking for jobs, they probably (and conservatively) have more than a few hundred thousand resumes of those looking for something better in their database. My key search word was "passion," and I searched everything: full time, part time, per diem, high school to advanced degrees, seasonal employees—the works. Any guesses as to how many of these résumés included the word "passion" on them, anywhere? Only 1,000. Roughly three-quarters of those received a High fit rating, meaning that the word was mentioned predominantly, and the remainder was split between a Medium and Low fit. The results were both fascinating and illuminating.

I randomly copied some of the seeker's Job Descriptions from both the first and last page of my "passion" search results:

- Customer service and call center manager
- High-performing clinical project manager
- Selfless nanny
- Account management professional with passion for media and Internet
- Bookkeeper (twice)
- Manufacturing/distribution clerical guru
- Experienced HR and music manager
- Senior RF design engineer

- High school English teacher
- Medical biller

The range of professions exhibited here spans media, biotech, education, various administration functions, engineering, and home care. This is critical to note because this scope of professions underscores a basic theme. You **can** be passionate about something work related, and the observation that not one but two bookkeepers appeared on the first page of "passion" results immediately makes this hypothesis a fact. Thank goodness there is a teacher who works with passion there, too! As we will explore, there is a much deeper link between your passions and what you like about your work. By identifying their drivers, your passions can be released and directed in a multitude of marvelous ways, depending on what is important to you at your current stage of life.

What is also extremely interesting about these results is the resoundingly low number of responses. Only roughly 750 résumés out of let's say, 500,000 on file (less than two-tenths of one percent) include the word "passion" on them in a primary context. What could this molecule in the pool be telling us? Three possibilities: First, those who aren't afraid to position themselves in such light might be finding employment more quickly than those who have reservations. My numerous recruiting functions have revealed that if you describe a passion on your résumé, aspects of it typically spring from the walls in the interview process. To quote a recruiting adage, "It isn't the most qualified candidate who gets the offer; it is the most passionate."

Second, the vast majority of job seekers might not quite know what they are passionate about in a work context (hence this book!). This ignorance coincidentally springs from the same source as their MBA peers: lack of experience, lack of focus or introspection, laziness, feeling the need to meet all sorts of expectations, or being fooled by the almighty title/income trap. Let me say here that these reasons should not be looked at as excuses or in any sort of derogatory light. People have been toying, torqueing, vexed, and tortured by this question for at minimum, our recorded history of time. Fortunately for today, our computers, algorithms, Ph.D.s, and various means of data collection can provide you with real-time, scientific, and mind-numbing reports confirming that a high percentage of workers aren't satisfied or happy with their jobs.

The last lesson that this small showing might impart is that if you are able to work your passions, you might not need Monster.com. This makes sense. Have you ever encountered people who simply love their work? They radiate a kind of energy that is both scintillatingly infectious and incredibly powerful. You want to hang out with them, sleep with them, or join their team. You want to understand how they tick and what their secret is. They probably also produce well above their standard peers, further reinforcing the attraction and draw—everyone wants to be associated with winners. In fact, the mere **feeling** that they are stoked about what they are doing can often fairly or unfairly influence perceptions of their performance.

Let's say you need to hire someone. Do you think this positive vibe and correlating performance make a difference? Do you think you will remember this person, track him down, and do whatever it takes to get a commitment? I worked with a woman in my first job out of graduate school who serves as a great case in point. She was always ready to do whatever was required to get the job done, always smiling, and upbeat even in the wee hours of the morning cranking out yet another last-minute deliverable with obnoxious, arrogant, and unhappy teammates. Even though the overriding culture of the organization was absolutely dismal, her performance was stellar. Three years later, I returned and hired her away to be one of the critical core team members of my Boston practice. Not surprisingly, she earned the highest bonus awarded to people at her level. Four years later, I pinged her again to see if she might be interested in working a particular gig. I can guarantee you she will **never** need Monster.com! (Sorry, Monster!)

BACK TO JACK

The flipside of this dynamic is also worthy of note. If you aren't happy with your job, how well do you think you can hide it? Believe it or not, your bosses and co-workers can easily tell if you are on the train. Let's suppose the unthinkable happens and the dark angel of downsizing makes an unexpected visit. Where on the must-keep list do you think you will fall if neither your heart nor your performance has been present in the business?

In fact, this is precisely why Mr. Welch imposed his 10% rule at General Electric—the lowest-performing 10% of your reports will be dismissed on a yearly basis, regardless of tenure. This is an extremely efficient way of doing a passion check with your employees, and GE's results bear this out. Mr. Welch was, in fact, doing his employees a huge favor by showing them the door—if GE doesn't have your attention and passion, neither your LifeTime nor the company's investment in you is being maximized. Light bulbs inevitably burn out.

To a significant degree, your ability to work your passions is another, though thankfully less lethal, manifestation of Darwin's Theory of Evolution. If you can align your passions and life, you will have a much easier LifeTime than those who don't. Not to beat a dead horse, but if you aren't happy in your working life (where you spend the majority of your LifeTime), to what extent does this unhappiness carry over to other parts of your LifeTime? Might it impact your relationships with significant others, kids, or pets? Could it negatively influence your demeanor, psyche, and personality? Ultimately, what does your gut and investment banker say unhappiness at work does to your overall health and longevity? Do you know anyone who has been miserable in work and who has died "young" of a stroke or cancer? I wouldn't go so far as to say "Only the passionate survive," but it would seem there is a tremendous degree of passion in those who have the strength to survive, endure, and enjoy as long a life as they want.

A great quote by Ken Chenault, CEO of American Express, from an interview in his college alumni magazine nicely sums up this chapter and foreshadows what is to come:

> "I think, at the end of the day, that it is a mistake simply to pursue a job. Instead, you should pursue a way of life. The opportunity for me is to make a fundamental difference in people's lives, both inside and outside the company. To lead a very successful enterprise that is not just focused on achieving business success. That's a consequence of doing the right things for our employees and our customers. The challenge of operating a global company is a terrific, terrific opportunity. You cannot be successful as a CEO in the short, moderate, or long term if you don't have a passion for what you're doing. The challenges and the issues are so substantial that if you don't have that passion, you're going to wilt. Fortunately, I think I've got that passion."

CHAPTER 5

A PROCESS OVERVIEW

THE PURPOSE OF THE FIVE PS

The process of the Five Ps has been designed to help you answer some simple yet historically elusive questions that fundamentally impact **every** detail of your daily affairs—**what** you do but more importantly **why**, in both grand and daily scheme, you are doing it. Autonomously, each P can facilitate potentially ground-breaking progress in your awareness of who you are, what you want from life, and how you can reach your goals. Combined, they present a compelling framework to enable you to live happily in the time of your life. The questions and their respective Ps follow:

1. What is your mission? **Passion**
2. What can the whole and impassioned you be the best at? **Proficiencies**
3. What is most important to you, where you are in Life? **Priorities**
4. How do you bring yourself to market? **Plan**
5. How do you fund your plan? **Prove**

The process has been designed with your journey front and center in mind. The first P focuses on figuring out the driving forces behind your journey. Without this purpose, pursuing life, liberty, and happiness can be inalienably frustrating and counterintuitive. Possessing even a sense of your meaning naturally triggers an accelerating and self-fulfilling alignment across your stars and planets, from your working life options to your social endeavors to your purposeful pastimes. The second P asks you to triangulate on the most powerful combination of innate skills, values, and experiences you can muster, equipping you with a custom-made walking stick, hand-crafted for your particular adventures. This is the "how" by which you optimally actualize your mission and passions, potentially in a variety of different settings as your LifeTime progresses.

The third P helps you define the importance of specific aspects of your journey, both now and in your future. This is why, in your "daily scheme" context, you choose to allocate your LifeTime to particular endeavors with the tacit understanding that as certain parts of your LifeTime evolve, other parts might also require transitioning. The fourth P provides a tactical roadmap for your excursion, replete with milestones and budgets. Generating this holistic plan before you start is obviously pragmatic—you certainly don't want to get lost en route to your promised land. Most importantly, this P lets you define the length and relative ruggedness of your particular path, based on your intrinsic openness to various sorts of risk—finances being a prime example.

The last P, which is arguably the most important depending on your circumstances, gives your outputs a test while soliciting whatever support you might need before you get cracking. For those whose income supports more than one outcome, getting buy-in for your plan is non-arguably essential. After that's secured, though, whatever next steps you need to make are trodden with the knowledge of a network, the confidence of confidantes, and the belief that belies any perceptions of potential failure.

THE POWER OF THE FIVE PS

You start by broaching the critical "why" question, which instills the tone for the entire process. It also kicks off your whirlpool, reaching out to the ends of your water's experiences and priorities, sucking them in, churning them a good number of times, yet all the while increasing their focus, energy, and applicability. Inevitably, from your vortex will emerge a tightly wound plan and means to support it.

In this context, combining answers to these questions can generate distinct insights into important realms of your journey. For example, combining the deliverables from the first two Ps can create some novel insights as to your life's work options.

PASSION + PROFICIENCIES = WORK OR "CAREER" OPTIONS

Instinctively, this formula makes sense. You should focus your working life in ways that combine your mission with what you love to do, are great at doing, and that fulfills a variety of experiences. In this context, please recall that the average American worker is currently pulling down four "careers" per LifeTime, and this number is only increasing. I must question the half-life of the term "career" since it denotes a life-long pursuit of success by rising through the ranks in a particular function or industry; the fact you are doing this four times on average either signifies the term is flawed or you have nine lives and purr.

Adding the second and third Ps provides a distinct view of how you can fundamentally prioritize your life and work.

PROFICIENCIES + PRIORITIES = WORK LIFE PRIORITIZATION

Understanding how your proficiencies can integrate with what is most important to you is obviously helpful as your LifeTime progresses. Working yourself silly (hopefully if you love what you are doing and are consequently kicking ass doing it) may suit you if that is your prime priority. Working the same schedule as other commitments/creatures start getting sucked up by your tornado might demand and even proactively cause your twister to slow down and quite possibly morph into a different sort of force.

Last, summing thoughts from the first three Ps create two powerful outputs. First are visions of potential journeys, both present and future, that you can explore or plan to start. Second, critical aspects of your niche—a work/life domain of your making and control—will appear. Identifying your niche is a primary purpose of the Five Ps. You will draw on and codify its supporting elements in the fourth P.

PASSION + PROFICIENCIES + PRIORITIES = JOURNEYS AND NICHE → PLAN

The Five Ps, like life, are iterative. You can derive an immense amount of insight and power by taking outputs from exercises and throwing them back into a prior tool or routine and running it again. To think you can simply sit down and nail things on a first, second, or even third pass may be a tad far-fetched; after all, we are talking about the entirety of your existence to date and the entirety of your existence until eternity—no small scale of inputs or degree of importance.

There is a final facet to the process that must be polished. At their core, the Five Ps hone your ability to focus your mind and efforts on a few particular yet key actions. Why is focus so important? Because life has a mischievous way of distracting you. There is always something else drawing your attention, always a multitude of other uses of your LifeTime, especially the small ones, which, like expenses, can quickly add up and even start to procreate. Just working at your computer and trying to avoid all the pop-ups, instant messages, the sound of e-mail arriving (which you simply have to open now!) alerts, schedule reminders, weather reminders, "put tick stuff on the cat" reminders, and so on can be immensely distracting. Of course, you can deactivate these bells and whistles, although a masochistic sliver of you might actually like the attention. Net sum: Generating whatever next steps you seek requires your unabashed focus.

The flipside of generating a plan is actually implementing it. It doesn't matter if your plan is as slick as silicone fluid—if you cannot execute it with the discipline of its author, its failure is assured. "Discipline" in this context does not necessarily imply "If you don't finish your work by 5:00 PM EST today, you will be required to stay after work and write the company mission statement on the whiteboard 50 times… in cursive." Discipline in our context simply means putting most distractions aside and following through on what you have created. To these ends, process outputs have been formulated for easy implementation because you will inevitably be sucked back into the maelstrom of mundane matters that are an unavoidable, although reducible, part of life.

Because this plan has been impassionedly designed by you and benefits you, attacking its execution with requisite discipline should be considerably easier than trying to follow prior directives where these elements were not evident. In addition, bear in mind that you decide whatever process results you want to actualize; if you only want to start with a few, that's cool. If you'd like to take the whole thing to the mat and pin it, go right ahead! To be clear, **you** are the **one** and **only** one who can ensure your plan is implemented to your standards. You can chuck a cat in water, but you can't make him drink!

A PRIMER ON THE FIVE PS

The Five Ps have been built to be flexible and to adapt as your life changes, **because it will.** Intrinsically, they ask that you take a step back from life from time to time or as certain events unfold, reassess where you are and what your current priorities are, and realign your LifeTime with the geography you are creating. Intuitively, this makes sense; experientially, it is a necessity. All its tools and exercises can be easily saved for future reference, reflection, and rerunning as your LifeTime evolves. Also, the Five Ps won't require reams of paper or complex organizational schemes to keep track of the moving parts. You might find yourself wanting or needing to go back and iterate on what you have done, and to these ends, using a computer to help you run, save, and rerun certain routines can be useful. This said, your trusty (and dusty?) pen and paper work just fine and have the advantage of immediate hand-scribbling, crossing-out, line-drawing, and so on.

Some additional notes are in order. I would like to disarm a minor threat you might be subconsciously or blatantly fearing: Supplying what the Five Ps need to do their job should **not** be difficult or require hours of incense/candle-lit meditation. Yes, there will be elements of PsychoBabbleMumboJumbo (which I have tried my best to diffuse as much as possible), and there will be some occasions where that dreadful chore of thinking charges in from stage right. Should any P ever become overly unruly, though, you are probably trying too hard. Let go, (count to ten), mellow, and go with the flow. Above all, the Five Ps should be easy, simple, and FUN to do.

The concepts supporting the Five Ps are not new. Every device has been used and abused before, albeit for slightly different purposes. To my knowledge, though, none of these business tools has ever been directed toward improving your personal life, which is perhaps a result of vain social attempts to keep the fragile work/life balance from crashing to the floor. It is the novel applications of these standard practices that gives the process its power, comprehension, and most importantly, ease of execution. Reading them in order probably makes some sense, although rigidly and sequentially performing them might not, depending on your desired uses. If, for example, all you are currently looking for is a way to make your current work a few degrees more passionate and a particular tool can help, use it. Although running through the entire process unquestionably yields the most powerful results, if you don't need to, just say no.

In fact, you might **not** want to dive in headfirst and go guns blazing through the Five Ps in one quick pass. Rather, you may want to digest the demands of each P first, jot down some notes, and simply think about the questions and their context in the process and your LifeTime. You may be surprised when and where both insights and applications intrude on your daily cycles: Sunday morning while lounging in bed reading the paper, on the golf course walking from green to tee, in the middle of a morning run or Stairmaster session, at a stop light en route to work, or in a hot steamy bath. Wherever they might happen, treat them similarly to X-Factors—embrace them and leverage and incorporate their value to the best of your ability.

THE TIPPING POINT

I would like to start closing this overview with a reference to a fascinating book by Malcolm Gladwell called *The Tipping Point*. The title, originally used to describe the dynamics of change in the racial composition of 1950's neighborhoods, centers on answering the question "What makes trends explode?" What causes ballistic growth of an idea, fad, or even biological reactions of all sorts— from teenage smoking, Hush Puppy shoe sales, and syphilis outbreaks to the success of the midnight ride of Paul Revere?

One of the book's main arguments is that whatever status quo is being examined, typically a few key drivers support that equilibrium. Imagine a safety net underneath a circus trapeze act supported by four wires, with each wire attached to a dial that controls its tautness. All it takes to trigger explosive growth or reaction is merely turning these knobs a few clicks—nothing major or revolutionary. Just a little fidgeting with the net can make the performers bounce much higher!

You can apply *The Tipping Point* thesis directly to your LifeTime. As the process reveals, your personal performance and happiness are driven primarily by three or four specific factors. You can probably list them without too much difficulty: rewarding work, good relationships with family and friends, meeting personal goals, and so on. In fact, you may be only a few iterations from experiencing tremendous growth in all facets of your life. The key to opening this lock is defining what these main drivers are and then figuring out which ones require how much fidgeting, bearing in mind you might need to try a few different combinations for the tumblers to fall just right.

The Five Ps have been designed with this theme in mind. You need not get lost in Nepal for six months to become enlightened (and simultaneously lightened of a fair chunk of change). Your itinerary might include a breathtaking hiking trip or a raucous whitewater rafting expedition, but please don't try to schedule "Universal Understanding," because the local guides will have little clue as to where to take you. All the Five Ps expects is that you start making small and iterative changes in key parts of your current daily cycle. Real change takes real time, and the best change can require a lot of time. Change can also be daunting and, in fact, downright nauseating because you are implicitly dealing with new and foreign terrain. Passionately going where you haven't gone before, with the courage and conviction of your core beside you, intuitively reduces the length of LifeTime required to meet your goals. Most importantly, you will be living on your terms!

SOME FINAL TIPPING POINTS

Before you push off, here are some additional facts and observations to preemptively deal with the natural reaction of "Hmm. This could take a bit of effort. Yeah, I'll read it, but I don't know when I'll get the time to actually do this." **The time is NOW**!

- Should you reach retirement age, you will have spent upward of **95,000** hours of your LifeTime working.
- You will also spend on average **2.2 years** of your LifeTime commuting to and from work—**2.2 years** of sleeping, making love, pursuing your life's work, watching movies or sports, playing sports, playing with your kids, vacationing, reading, and however else you like to use your time.

I fervently hope you spend these nontrivial chunks of LifeTime in the pursuit of something passionate.

You might well go on to realize more financial gain than you ever dreamt possible. However, you might not, and there is **nothing** wrong with this.

If you aren't married, you might. Then again, you might not. If you do, looking purely at the numbers, there is a greater than 50% chance that this relationship won't last, and, if you have kids, a roughly similar probability that you will experience personal bankruptcy.

You might be blessed by the greatest gift life can give you— children. You might try every conceivable means possible and for reasons beyond your control, be unable to bear them.

You will probably lose a friend from high school within the next three years. (My wife lost her junior prom date to cancer last year.)

You might lose a parent in the next three years. (My father was diagnosed with an advanced stage of colon cancer more than ten years ago.)

You might retire to Florida, Arizona, or some other warm climate to enjoy your "golden years" walking the water's edge, pants rolled up above your ankles, sipping a glass of Chardonnay, as depicted in airline magazines' advertisements. Odds are, you probably won't.

If there is one steadfast belief that protrudes from this swirling backdrop of chance, it's this: By believing in your core and pursuing your passion, you can *happily* live in the time of your life. The process of the Five Ps is a valiant effort to help you actualize this endeavor.

ARE YOU READY?

CHAPTER 6

THE FIRST P: PASSION

WHAT DO YOU WANT YOUR TOMBSTONE TO SAY?

So... what's your passion? What gets you going like **nothing** else? How do you even define "passion"? I have posed this last question to a variety of audiences over the years, and some of the most topical responses consistently come from young urban adults enrolled in a cutting-edge nonprofit organization called YearUp. I usually try to capture their responses on large sticky pads I have been saving over time. A few selections follow:

"Something you just love to do... something that no one would have to pay you to do."

"Something that is at your core, a part of you."

"Passion is what keeps us going. It provides life."

"It is like living to my favorite song... you know where it is going before it even gets there."

"Something you can't shake... that is with you from the moment you wake up until the moment you go to sleep."

"Something you care so much about you would die for it."

I absolutely adore and respect these ad-hoc descriptions because their superficial simplicity masks backgrounds that might have already needed to confront their cores. The last one really strikes at the heart of what you are seeking—something you can happily give your every last ounce of strength to fulfill, or perish trying.

These descriptors also share a broad applicability, which is where we will start the process of discovering two interlocking concepts key to this P: your mission and what I call your meta-passions. Your **mission** is a straightforward statement encapsulating what you have been born to do—*what you are passionate about, can be the best at, and love to do*. **Meta-passions** buttress your mission. They represent the *essence* of what you would do with your life if you only had a year to live. They are the why behind the statements "I love to volunteer" (helping others), "I love to mountain bike" (pushing and challenging myself), "I love teamwork" (being a part of something), "I love art" (creating perspective), "I love making love" (sharing pleasure), "I love to cook" (making others feel good), or "I love my kids" (being crawled on).

The importance of particular meta-passions may wax and wane as your experiences accumulate and priorities change. They might also transcend many experiences. For example, you may not have realized the innate enjoyment you receive from helping others grow and succeed from sharing knowledge, but it certainly explains why over the past ten years you enrolled in mentor programs, became certified to lead courses, and stayed late working on your Chinese workmate's English pronunciation skills. Again, a key thing to remember is that your meta-passions are inextricably linked to your mission.

Combined, these random genetic and environmental factors permeate every protein in your body. They get you out of bed in the morning, gnaw on your commute, shadow you throughout the day, laugh at you during those pathetically long-winded meetings, reflect you in the eyes of your kids as you raise them, invade your daydreams, rattle your head as you exercise, push your expectations, and finally, provide the calming reassurance you are alive and in control as you drift asleep. Any bells ringing here?

Even if you are a die-hard masochist (or investment banker), *innately*, you desire to work your passions. And in this context, you are probably much closer than you think to realizing, actualizing, and monetizing yours. It is merely a matter of distilling your vat of experiences, purifying the outputs, and identifying their concentrate *with no preference to satisfying a pre-existing desired flavor*. Your mission and meta-passions typically sit right under your nose, so close you would trip over them if they were suddenly to materialize. Their invisible mystery hides inside the obvious fact that no one to date probably has sat you down and asked you these specific questions.

You already have at least one mission in you, and possibly more, depending on what X-Factors—good and bad—have or will grace you. You have a purpose of your making, and although X-Factors may help you realize, change, or refine your mission(s), *your core is not and will never be empty*. The real question becomes this: "How do you meet your mission using your meta-passions, given your strengths and present and future priorities?" This physical fulfillment of your mission and meta-passions is what I call your **releases**. For example, working as a fireman would be a release of a meta-passion to put your life on the line, which supports a mission to save other's lives. Your releases surround you because they essentially are how you choose to allocate your LifeTime. They're where you live, the kind of books you love to read, the kind of movies you love to see, your musical tastes, the kind of work you enjoy. They can manifest in the kind of car you drive, the clothes you wear, your circles of friends, and where and how you like to travel. The list goes on and on. Implicitly, how you choose to spend your LifeTime reflects the releases of your mission and meta-passions.

Figure 6.1 maps out how three critical factors interact. At the top, you have your mission, tightly linked with your meta-passions. Continuing down, these meta-passions (and thus your mission) are expressed by your releases. In this context, your meta-passions serve to channel the energy of your mission to particular releases.

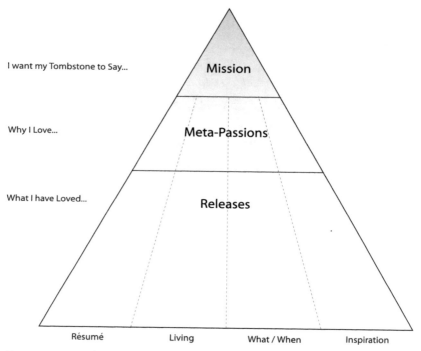

FIGURE 6.1   Looking for patterns in your experiences.

This chapter helps you start the process of iterating toward understanding the top and driving parts of this graphic. Developing a mission statement right off the bat is possible, although including content from the next P, Proficiencies, can be tremendously helpful. In other words, don't worry if your mission doesn't come blazing off your pencil or screen immediately.

THE PATTERNS OF YOUR EXPERIENCES

To make this process work, we will be using a brainstorming technique that is extraordinarily useful in everything from running marketing focus groups and assessing aspects of organization's cultures to developing new branding campaigns. Basically, you will be looking for patterns in and between certain sets of data. Although this might sound like it requires a master's degree in analytical extrapolation, all you need to do is approach the process with a clear and open mind to make it work. Generating this data simply entails answering some clear-cut questions and your first pass consists of only four quick steps that can be completed easily in less than 20 minutes. Are you ready?

STEP 1: CONSTRUCT THE FRAMEWORK

Like most effective brainstorming processes, you will need something to draw on, and the larger this something is, the more prolific your thoughts and better results you can typically expect.[1] For this exercise, draw a pyramid just like the one previously displayed. Ignore, for the moment, the top level (mission and meta-passions), and divide the bottom level (releases) into four sections with the headings Résumé, Living, What/When, and Inspiration.

The first key question you will be answering is "What have I loved about particular life experiences to date?" This said, although it is considerably easier to triangulate on your passions directly rather than deductively, immense insight can come from exploring why you **disliked** certain aspects of the same experiences. If you'd like to include these inputs into this process, simply lengthen the legs of the pyramid a bit and horizontally divide the Releases section into likes and dislikes, as in Figure 6.2.

---

1. Although a whiteboard or those large sticky pads are fantastic if you can get your hands on them, a random yellow pad works, too.

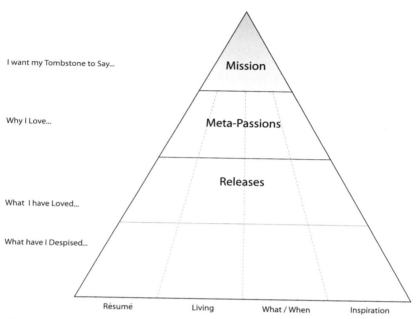

FIGURE 6.2   Pyramid with likes and dislikes.

STEP 2: IDENTIFY YOUR RELEASES

This is the main data-generation step of this exercise. This is where you explore your life's experiences with a magnet charged to attract those glittering streaks of passion that logically pervade your mountain. Let's start drilling into the topics referenced earlier—résumé, living, what/when, and inspiration—to extract their pertinent data. Remember: This is not actual mining, so no blasting is required!

Résumé

The best cauldron to start boiling is your dreaded résumé. Don't worry if your previous version was punched out on a Smith Corona typewriter. Résumés typically consist of three main parts: Work, Education, and Other Pursuits. For this section, we will focus on the first two. Ignore all your many and varied accomplishments, and zero in on what you loved about your relevant experiences from both sections—"relevant" meaning those experiences in which there was something that memorably stoked your passion fires. You might even consider (boldly) going off-résumé and including summer or part-time jobs, internships, and even something as incidental as babysitting if there was something about it that triggered a passion. You might want to locate a list of employers and educators against the left side of your Releases section and then ask yourself the following questions:

- What did you love about working for Employer A? What about the experience—your role, your department, the company, the entire industry—were you proud to tell the world about?
- What did you love about going to school at College G? What about its spirit, size, philosophy, students, and so on resounded with you?
- What sort of extracurricular opportunities did you zealously pursue in either sphere? Did you play a sport or two, develop a penchant for debating, or get involved in a community outreach program through Employer C?

Now, no matter how wacky or seemingly off the mark your responses may seem, write them down in the appropriate space. This is critical, because the more data points you can muster, the deeper and easier your patterns will be to discern. Try to keep your answers concise, but if you need to ramble, ramble on!

Similarly, if you chose to run the "dislikes" routine, reflect on what you found absolutely uninspiring and nauseating about certain experiences, and write it down. You can copy the list template from earlier, although you might need to alter it because not all releases necessarily have passionate or despicable features.

Living

This is where the Other or Additional Pursuits section of your résumé kicks in. Hopefully, your description of these activities on your résumé **fully** represents what you absolutely love to do when you're not at work (or perhaps what you secretly think about while working and coincidentally have adorned your walls with). If not, simply (re-) ask yourself this question: "If I had only a year to live, how would I spend it?" Again, it could be taking pictures of flowers, sailing to exotic far-away places, teaching people to make pottery, or creating the best growth portfolio the investment world has ever encountered. The kind of sports you love to play, volunteer efforts, musical preferences, and so on can convey volumes about the way your core has been crafted and possibly how your mission might materialize. A simple trick to this whole process may merely be infusing your Work Experiences with the impassioned force behind your Other Pursuits and looking for ways to move these pursuits into the main section of your résumé.

What/When

There is a fair degree of consensus in the psychological research community that what you liked to do when you were an adolescent is reflected in what floats your boat professionally. For boys, the magic age is approximately 12, and for girls, 11. This makes intuitive sense. You have amassed over a decade of experiences, have a decent although probably unconscious idea of your strengths and weaknesses, and your parents have given you the freedom to sample different releases—all before those pesky puberty hormones mess everything up!

A brilliant example of this correlation recently surfaced at an address to my local Boy Scout troop. I mentioned this link to the kids, many of whom were right at that target age. After the presentation, I was talking with a man whose son was in the troop. He was a Wharton grad named Fred who had gone into real estate finance and consulting after graduation. After about five years of this abuse, one day he and his wife both told their respective employers they were simply getting off their trains. The senior partners at their respective firms were ecstatic they had the will to stop. The junior partners were nervously puzzled. "What are you going to do?" was a common refrain. Verbally reflecting, Fred recounted, "When I was 12, I loved to build things… in fact, the most pleasure I got in high school and college was constructing sets for plays and performances." They returned to the Boston area, and now this Wharton grad is happily building things once again—cabinets, kitchens, desks, whatever you need. If it is made from wood, Fred can build it, probably better than most, and he does a great deal of his work from home. He is even thinking of going back to school to further hone his craft.

Think back, and if you can't zero in on anything solid, don't worry. The important task is planting the seed. When your memory does latch on to something, write it down.

Inspiration

Conjure up a list of say two or three people who really inspire you, and think about why you find them motivating. They can be anyone: your mother, a famous athlete, a college professor, a favorite writer or filmmaker, a business titan, a socio/political change agent, or a friend you went to school with so many years ago. Your reasons could be anything from living a bold life, dedicating a LifeTime to a particular pursuit, taking a stand against prejudice, or winning the race after overcoming a major obstacle. Please refrain, though, from focusing on the usual reason associated with commerce kingpins—"Bill Gates, because he has made a ton of dough." These inputs can provide significant guidance in defining your meta-passions and even your mission. Conceptually, what excites you about others' stories can often resemble how you want to excite your passions.

STEP 3: BRAINSTORM TO IDENTIFY POTENTIAL META-PASSIONS

Take your release scribbles (and possibly a nice drink or pot of tea) and look for patterns within and between the sections. Ask yourself, "Why have I loved my past and current releases? Why have I allocated my LifeTime (and finances) to these ends?" These patterns are typically recurring themes: a yearning to understand; a lust to help others; a proclivity to inform; a deep-seeded desire to create; a life-long obsession with a particular sport, activity, or vocation; or possibly, an inexplicable need to change the world around you. Although the majority of your data is probably fighting for space in the Résumé and Living sections, don't discount for a moment the power that the What/When and Inspiration sections can add to this mix.

When these patterns start taking shape, start plugging and playing your thoughts into the middle layer of the pyramid, and don't hesitate to make radical changes to your entries as your ideas churn. You can probably generate two or three rather quickly, although you may want to leave a little space for additional realizations that might come as your pencil dust settles. Not surprisingly, the easiest identifiable meta-passions typically emerge from your living section, and it is not uncommon for only faint reflections to shine from your résumé data. Draw lines, in different colors if you'd like, connecting these patterns to their respective meta-passions, as in Figure 6.3.

There will be some releases for which no glaring meta-passion exists. This is not atypical or unexpected because certain releases might frankly be outliers or ghosts in your machinery. Or perhaps they are part of another pattern whose supporting points might not have been included yet. What is fascinating about these seemingly random releases is that oftentimes they can add tremendous value in defining a meta-passion and closing in on your mission.

The First P: Passion

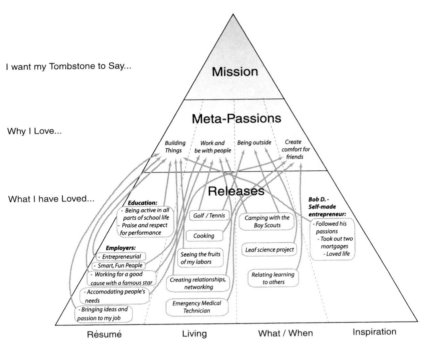

FIGURE 6.3   Diagram of filled-in pyramid.

For example, I absolutely love admissions work (aka hiring). I worked for the admissions departments in both undergraduate and graduate school and oversaw the Los Angeles admissions committee for five years out of undergrad. Not surprisingly, this fiber continued to my corporate years, culminating in an effort to recruit 100 colleagues in under a year. Yet this love hadn't appeared on my résumé for years (like the fact that I was the Opinions Editor for my graduate school newspaper).

Going through the pyramid process, these releases quickly coalesced into a meta-passion I hadn't considered—a yearning to help people live happy lives by introducing them to my alma maters and employers. This meta-passion filled in a missing gap that helped seal the realization of my mission. Give your memory box another spin to see if you can supplement any lone-standing releases with other data points from whatever corners of your past. And remember, although you have segmented your pyramid into four sections, they are all life.

If you have chosen to work with the dark side of your force, use this same process for your "dislike" releases, trying to identify your "anti-passions" at the bottom of the pyramid. Again, this process can be reinforcing and fulfilling primarily because it provides additional information you can use to distance your meta-passions and mission from the clutter of the world.

STEP 4: LOOK FOR PATTERNS FROM TOP TO BOTTOM AND BOTTOM TO TOP

What **do** you want your tombstone to say? Look across your meta-passions. Are there any consistent themes at play here between them? Include your releases from right to left. Anything leap at you with the conviction of historical fact that you were born to fulfill a particular goal? There might be; there might not. Again, conceptually, your mission should include inputs from the next P, so don't worry if nothing blatantly jumps out of your scribbles just yet. This is an excellent example of the need to iterate to make this process work. Even if something appears at this point, it will more than likely require further refining, time, thought, patience, and a couple burnishes by your mental cloth before its grand debut.

What you are looking for is that single blanket that connects and envelops both your meta-passions and releases. It could be an inexplicable fascination and desire to promote the game of badminton. It could be a deep-seeded desire to end world hunger. It could be servicing customers unlike no one before you. It could be something as simple as wanting to provide the best LifeTime for your kids. Simultaneously, it could very easily be an existing meta-passion or perhaps how you have defined a particularly important release. This happens frequently, particularly if you have already consciously started thinking about these questions at some point in your LifeTime. Again, this is not a MENSA test; your answers may be unshakably staring you in the face. If you are able to identify something, fill in the triangle. This is Version 1.0 of your mission.

Here's a little additional commentary about this mission concept, which might both cloud and clarify your search. I believe, at your core, that you want to improve the world around you in some small or large way. You don't want to die anonymously. It could be by donating money, material, or your time to a charity or even working for one. (Approximately 85% of philanthropic donations, which exceeded $200 billion in 2003, came from the general public.) It could be by advancing technologies to benefit the world in amazing ways. It could be by growing or protecting free markets and democracy. It could be marketing a product you believe can truly improve people's lives. It could be something as simple as wanting to raise happy, confident children, which may be the most difficult yet most productive and fulfilling investment of a LifeTime that can be made. Regardless of the "how," though, thinking of your mission in terms of "I want to improve the world by…" *might* make the process a little easier. Looking at your mission in this context, much like the missions that pepper our literary and cinematic histories, can add another layer of importance and (dare I say) *immortality* to your daily endeavors.

THE KID FACTOR

On this note of wanting to live forever, there is a fundamental biological component that can influence or downright alter the top of your pyramid—having hooligans. I have had many conversations with women who, after reviewing and describing what they like to do, are surprised to realize their mission, deep down, is simply to be the best Mommy the world has ever known. I have similarly had conversations with men, who after a much longer look at their likes/dislikes, confess (typically post-birth) their meta-passions and even missions have changed or widened to include being the best father the world has ever seen. We will drill down much further in this topic in the third P; however, I'd like to relate a few observations about this particularly magical X-Factor.

First, it is absolutely, unconditionally, **completely** groovy to state a mission in this context; don't let this zeitgeist's expectations lead you anywhere your gut doesn't find palatable. In fact, providing futures of a variety of sorts for your kids is probably the strongest and most enduring mission you can ever undertake—a safer world, cleaner environment, financial resources, education—this rubric can easily become all-encompassing. "Why am I working so hard? Because I want the best _____ for my kids!" Melding your mission with these muscles can quickly and clearly align your interests, making the process of figuring out how you want to release your LifeTime that much easier to chart and actualize.

Second, having hooligans **is** a major life-altering event that fundamentally impacts how you spend your LifeTime—where you live, your social groupings, your schedule, cash flow, and possibly even the kind of work you want to do to support these new lives. Calling it an X-Factor may or may not be completely true; however, from a world-rocking perspective, family expansion ranks very, very high.

These observations about kids underscore a deeper point: Certain events can shake your entire pyramid all the way from mission to releases. They can be abrupt and cathartic; they can be subliminal and slow. Regardless of their origin, be aware that they can and very well might happen just when you least expect them, and if they do, be ready to recognize and embrace them. The **last** thing you want to do is fashion a set of releases based on a faulty mission!

CASE STUDY: VALERIE

To justly bring Valerie to life (and into yours), a brief background is in order. She is in her late 30s and has seen a lot of life so far. She comes from a professional family on Boston's North Shore and received a sterling education growing up. Her parents divorced a few years back, and one has remarried. Hitched in her mid-twenties but then quickly divorced, she has enjoyed a relatively "successful" software and services sales career, which has allowed her to live in the San Francisco Bay area, Chicago, and most recently, back in the Boston suburbs. It has also provided her with a decent cushion of savings.

I met Valerie when I hired her to lead sales in some particular verticals during one of my turnarounds, and we have kept in touch since. Having been in sales for the past 15 years, she has tired of playing the quota game and was in the process of considering outright resigning from her current employer. She was looking at some different options in the software space, although only for the short to medium term until she could figure out what her next big steps might be. "I want to be doing something to improve the world on my terms." She is an active volunteer and serves on a couple of local nonprofit boards. She recently bought a nice townhouse with views of the ocean from her top floor. She absolutely loves it, although making the mortgage payment while maintaining a comfortable standard of living is a monthly concern. She is looking to make some fairly large changes in her life long term.

Valerie finished the first iteration of her brainstorm in less than 20 minutes with no clear mission emerging from the mist of pencil detritus. A cleaned-up version appears in Figure 6.4. Note how many of her releases connect directly to her meta-passions! Also note how her living releases provide other potential work options, her proficiencies notwithstanding.

continues

Case Study: Valerie (continued)

An important expectation was just mentioned that deserves a little more ink. When you start this exercise, please try your hardest **not** to enter it with a particular mission in mind. The human ability to assemble data to meet a predefined hypothesis is extraordinary and likewise can produce extraordinary failure. Again, remember the Stockdale Paradox: We are merely looking for the honest facts because only they can inevitably provide you with the basis for effective change.

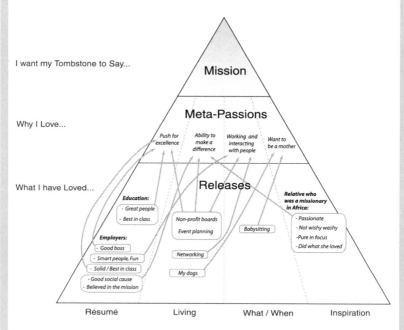

Figure 6.4   Diagram of Valerie's passion graphic.

Making a Stand

It has become increasingly difficult (maybe I'm just getting older here) to wear your emotions on your sleeve, sport a Pro-fill-in-the-blank hat in public, or put on your passions with pride. For the process to really have effect, you must treat your mission—whatever it might be—as if it were your spouse or significant other. There's no embarrassment in making the proper introductions in social settings, and no holding grudges or socking away complaints. You will need to constantly talk things through, and you must be willing to spend literally years of your LifeTime on the relationship. You would be willing to throw yourself in the path of an oncoming train to save your mission and would follow it barefoot and in tatters to the ends of the earth, death on hold, to embrace it just once more. Most metaphorically, you should be able to seek a similar degree of solace, support, love, and energy from your mission as you receive from this special and fortunate person. There will be days when you will say to yourself, "Why on earth am I doing what I am doing right now?" Being able to look to something so powerful and personal is an extraordinary gift.

How Do I Know?

"You know, Lawler, I have gone through your first P and have gained some great insights regarding my mission, and I think I am very close to nailing the top of my pyramid shut. How can I be sure, though, that what I have come up with is right?" I have two observations to respond to this very pragmatic question.

#1: Trust Your Gut

It's fascinating to observe how much of our education system—MBA programs being a prime example—are geared toward providing a statistically proven set of formulas to serve as **panaceas** for our problems when our guts, in truth of fact, can often be an equal or better bellwether. I have a great personal story to illustrate this point. I had the pleasure of interviewing the Corporate Alliance Marketing demi-god for Sun Microsystems, a pivotal role to Sun's overall strategy and revenue streams. The purpose of our conversation was to understand the process he used to determine how Sun's partners were selected. I will never forget his lead-off response, "You know something... we run all sorts of analyses—discounted free cash flow, risk assessments, scenario planning, et cetera... but the reason why Sun pays me the big bucks is to trust my gut." I can recall being more than a little mystified at the time. Here he was, a man responsible for hundreds of millions of dollars in revenue each year telling me he used his internal compass as the key deciding factor as to with whom Sun should partner.

By all means, use whatever data you have at your disposal—information can be extremely valuable. At the same time, though, do a quick gut check; if you find your stomach churning, give your data another good once-over. There is a distinct and crucial difference between the natural discomfort of going **in** a new direction and lacking comfort **with** a new direction; instinctively, you want the former.

#2: LIFE IS AN ITERATIVE PROCESS

Life, like software development, is an iterative process. There will always be bugs even after your second or third version's release. "Character consists of what you do on the third and fourth tries," says noted novelist James Michener. The critical component that must sit at the core of your life rules is the need to iterate. Learn from your experiences, try like hell to document these learnings, and then infuse them into your next effort.

The First P: Passion

A participant at a business school presentation was noticeably upset and uncomfortable by this concept. He interrupted with a curt blurt, "So what you are telling me is that I may have to try three or four different jobs before I find my sweet spot? This doesn't make sense at all. It seems like a big waste of time and effort." I then asked the audience how many different "career paths" the average American worker currently commences over the course of his working life. Silence loomed as all the marketing students tried to recall the latest census figures. Then someone far in the back spoke up with the confidence of fact, "I believe it is around four presently, although it is projected to go higher."

"You are correct," I replied. "So the question becomes do you want to use these shifts to continually narrow down on your passions, or do you want to make these changes merely for the trendy hell of it?"

It is time to move to the next P!

CHAPTER 7

THE SECOND P: PROFICIENCIES

WHAT CAN THE WHOLE AND IMPASSIONED YOU BE THE BEST AT?

Imagine an inverted funnel, sitting on a table. The height of the funnel represents your ability to perform and excel in all aspects of life. You have been able, through brute force, education, late nights, and so on to scratch your way up to just about where the funnel becomes vertical. Now, every once in a while you meet people who are obviously operating at the top of the funnel, dancing on a completely different plane. They love what they are doing so much that you perceive there is no difference to them between their work and life. They are masters of their domain. They are the gurus, the authorities CNN calls when an appearance is needed for a story related to their particular line of work.

The obvious question is this: How do you scale that funnel's spout? What can enable you to be the absolute best at what you do? The answer is rooted in four critical and perhaps seemingly adversarial questions:

- What am I innately good at doing?
- What do I absolutely love to do?
- What are my personal values?
- What life experiences do I want to leverage and fulfill?

These four questions deal with all the aspects of your life that are critical to working life, not merely working a job. Each is important on its own; when combined, a synergy of immense insight and power can be created. What is important to note is that conceptually, combining these outputs with your meta-passions (and eventually mission) provides the detailed and personalized information you need to investigate specific work options. Let's explore the rationales for these questions.

WHAT I AM INNATELY GREAT AT DOING?

You have been blessed with a unique set of characteristics and valuable capabilities. At the same time, you blatantly lack or need to improve others, which is nothing to fret about. You are human after all! In fact, you may not be aware of what your strengths and weaknesses truly are, and perhaps more importantly, what your strengths and weaknesses are **as perceived by others and in certain contexts**. You may have been working in situations where employee growth and development is a corporate fallacy or whose systems and processes tend to focus on how to improve your deficiencies, versus leveraging your strengths. Similarly, you might be innately great at a particular function, but for a variety of reasons—corporate culture, industry, your boss—your capabilities have lost their luster.

The more time you spend burnishing your strengths, the better your performance and overall contribution will be to whatever endeavor you have undertaken. The thought that you can become a super-all-around-achiever seems fundamentally misguided in this context. Yes, you can do a decent job at most things, but wouldn't it be better to create extraordinary results in one or two particular functions and let others do the same in their specific domains?

The Second P: Proficiencies

This boils down to the notion of teamwork, which resurfaces in the fourth P.

A Chinese parable called "The Waterbearer" illustrates this point nicely. Two earthen pots were selected to carry water from a stream to a nearby town. They were balanced at opposite ends of a fairly long wooden stick that the waterbearer would dip into the nearby stream and then place across his shoulders to return to the town. One of the clay pots was cracked, though, and by the time the waterbearer reached his destination, only half of its water was present. After about a year, the cracked pot asked the waterbearer why he was using it, because it only delivered half of what its counterpart was able to transport. The waterbearer smiled and asked the cracked pot if it had seen the beautiful flowers that had blossomed underneath it as it traveled back to town. Yes, replied the cracked pot. I have seen them. The waterbearer then confided that he had known about the cracked pot's uniqueness and had spread flower seeds under its path; if it weren't for the cracked pot's ability to provide water to the seeds, the flowers that made his job enjoyable would never have existed.

This proverb exposes two important points. First, by letting the pot be itself, it was able to serve a purpose that it was **uniquely** qualified to perform. Second, what may seem like a weakness or a need for improvement can actually be incredibly powerful **in the right context**. Please bear this in mind as you start the upcoming exercise—specifically, what you may have been dinged on in prior reviews might merely be due to a difference in managerial style, personality, or lack of consistent expectations, if they were set at all. Trust your gut here!

I have a final observation that carries over to the next question. You may not have had enough experience in different capacities and contexts to be able to definitively pinpoint what you're innately good at doing. Part of this issue might be resolved in the way your full data set is collected, as described later in this chapter. For now, don't stop being curious about what options are out there. The only boxes you need to think outside of are ones you create, which you can just as easily destroy. Talk to people. Ask them to share their stories, observations, likes, and dislikes in the context of different functions. Lastly, be patient. Life is an iterative process, and unless you are really lucky, it will take water from more than a couple of trips to grow your proverbial flowers.

WHAT DO I ABSOLUTELY LOVE TO DO?

This question is a blatant no-brainer. To be the best, you must be both exceptional at something and **love** to perform that something. This may sound simple to determine. However, answering this question might require a couple of thought rotations to get your mind outside of your current working confines. "Yes, I am good, in fact I think **really** good, at managing IT projects, but do I **really** love doing it?" A hypothetical question you can use to help determine this is asking yourself, "If I were to die doing something, would _____ be on my top five list of things I'd want to be doing?"

This question might also be difficult to answer because it runs head on into how your success is defined at work and in life. Theoretically, the employee review process consists of expectations being set, metrics being defined to assess your performance, and then quantitative and qualitative judgments of your results. Presuming your career path has been based predominantly on what you are good at, a decent probability exists that you might not absolutely love what has been identified as your main strengths. Yes, you have been able to "succeed" doing XYZ functions and have risen through the ranks based on them. Looking back, a significant issue you may have already encountered is that the amount of energy you find yourself needing to spend on maintaining your success has increased *lockstep* with your career trajectory. Intuitively and inevitably, situations like these cannot last. If you love what you do and are great at it, getting caught in mudslides like this can be minimized.

A classic example of this occurs in sales. Some of the most gifted salespeople lead utterly miserable lives because at their core, they don't like to sell. They have been lured into this profession by money or "the rush of the deal" and can perform well, the whole while hating what they are doing. While their "success" grows, so do their numerical targets to exceed to get that President's-Club-Gold-Plate-of-Superior-Excellence-Award status. Oh yeah, do you think their monthly fixed costs might start edging up as their commissions grow? It is a natural human tendency to start projecting a repeat of last month's or quarter's performance when thinking about that trade-up mortgage or car payment. Heard of any salespeople who have become chemically dependent because of dealing with these pressures?

Realizing that your career successes to date may have been based on something less than your full potential can be extremely frustrating and simultaneously liberating. The most difficult part of this process is figuring out how to make the transition to that magic combination of being great at what you love to do because it might or might not exist in your current workplace. If it does, it may require a salary reduction, a lower title, and dealing with the perceived social stigma of taking an unorthodox career jump. "Yeah, John, he just couldn't cut it in marketing. I have no idea why he suddenly joined HR; they are such a bunch of idiots."

The process can get even trickier if you realize your current working situation does not harbor the opportunity for you to harness your desired skills. How do I find another opportunity that will value my natural love? How do I explain to my parents or significant other why I need to leave my current job? Both of these questions are answered in upcoming stages of the 5Ps, but for the moment, don't panic. In fact, be happy; it will soon become apparent that by aligning your skills with your passions, your performance **and** career will quickly gather momentum and start to snowball in seemingly magical ways.

WARNING! SELLER BEWARE!

A general warning is now in order. As previously stated, you have already been iterating unconsciously toward a career based on your passions. You might have even found the right role, but something still is not hunky-dory. What is missing is the context of your work. A good magnification of this syndrome can be seen in the story of my good friend Keith.

Keith's skills and passion selling his company's service offerings were legendary. He worked his tail off, even in industries that were not his strength, and he put together teams and proposals that consistently won business. He flourished. Keith, I quickly realized, is your typical rock star sales stud, the kind of salesperson who could sell nicotine patches at a tobacco grower's convention.

That company unfortunately got hit hard by the economy, and Keith eventually got involved selling some financial backend software. For various reasons, he hated it. Every time we spoke, he kept complaining about how his heart just wasn't in this one, how he was missing his wife and recently born son as he traveled all over the country selling stuff he really didn't care about. In typical fashion, he was making and beating his numbers. However, happy he was not. "I hate this job," he would lament. "I just got out of a two-hour sales call, and I don't remember a word that was said. I don't feel like I am adding value here at all. Yeah, I'm making some random accountant's job easier, but is that important to me? Not in the slightest."

Keith had been looking around for other opportunities, and a friend had just started running a vitamin/health care business and had been trying to get Keith on board. "Now vitamins—they make people feel better. THAT is something I can get behind!" he said enthusiastically. Keith, of course, was concerned about his income stream petering down during the transition. "Look, Keith," I pointed out, "Yes, you will notice an immediate drop in income. How long before you return to your current level is unknown. One thing is for certain, though. If you are passionate about what you are selling, three key things will happen: Your downtime will undoubtedly be shortened, perhaps dramatically, and more importantly, when you hit your upside, you will hit it with a vengeance. Your results will start clearing the fences with such drive, someone will make a mint selling windshield insurance to the folks who parked their cars behind center field."

"Most importantly, the amount of **your** time to make this happen will substantially decrease. I mean, imagine being able to spend half the energy and frustration you currently do to make your numbers on work that will yield better financial **and** family dividends?" In short, Keith knows what he loves to do and is exceptionally good at it **when his heart is behind what he is selling**. He has become trapped by his own "success." As he keeps meeting his numbers, the bar will go higher and will require even more sacrifice of his LifeTime to meet and exceed expectations the next time around. He hasn't left his current employer yet (their second child recently arrived), although the seeds have definitely been sown.

The critical nuance here is that it may not be your function you don't like; it is how you are using what you are innately great at that is the obstacle. You could be marketing a consumer product when your passions are geared toward financial services. You could be a programmer, stuck in an oil and gas consulting firm, who wants to beat cancer. You could be a nurse in Sioux City, Iowa with an innate lust to roam the world and who has just learned about Doctors Without Borders or that cruise lines need nurses. Context is key!

WHAT ARE MY VALUES?

This is one of the most important yet unattended topics in life—living with those squishy things called values. In our quest for material dominance, we have the unfortunate tendency to sell both our souls and values, and very quickly at that. You probably don't even realize where you have unconsciously placed your values in the overall prioritization of "what is important about this job to me?" Give this a little thought: How can you ever be happy working in an environment that, at its core, does not support your values? Do you think your productivity and overall demeanor might noticeably suffer?

At the beginning of the day, your values emanate from your core. They are intractable, immutable to the point where trying to remove them from your daily life resembles the vain attempt to part the clutched fist of a tired and surly daughter from her soggy cotton candy wand. So why are values ignored in the quest for the offer or the opportunity to work for XYZ sexy employer? First, you more than likely don't even know precisely what your values are. When was the last time anyone sat you down and asked you to list your values? Have you ever seen them on a résumé? Is there a Monster.com field for values? Second, it can be difficult to be open about something so close to you. You probably don't relish the opportunity of opening your kimono to the world in such an unabashed manner. You might come off as obnoxious, arrogant, or even worse, off-topic, wimpy, or out to lunch. "Why should you want to share your values with me?" thinks Mr. Hiring Manager. "Why should I care?"

Throughout my recruiting experiences, only rarely have I fielded questions from candidates looking to understand the nuances and reality of the company's mission and values to assess whether their personal versions adequately overlap to make the experience truly **mutually** beneficial. This is extremely disheartening. To be fair, many companies that have publicly presented "values" have hired consulting firms to develop and bring them to market merely as window-dressing. Instilling values into an organization, particularly one that has been managed (or mismanaged) for many years without them, can be an extremely difficult process. It took Jack Welch, Mr. Cheerleader Extraordinaire, many years to feel he had been able to properly express and inculcate his desired set of values into all layers of the GE bureaucracy and workforce. And that is only half the battle from his or any employer's perspective. "Now I've gotta make sure my employees' values are **in alignment** with those values of the company!" Looking at GE's extraordinary results, the process of defining and aligning values should receive considerable attention on **both** sides of the W-2 filing process.

To what degree do you don your Dr. Jekyll suit when you go to work and then, somewhere in the commute home, re-emerge as Mr. Hyde? How much LifeTime, how much energy might you waste going through these daily metamorphoses to bring in that higher salary or bigger bonus when a major component of this dissatisfaction is blatantly gnawing on your core? I see it on a daily basis, on the subways, on the highways, on the commuter trains, and even more apparently on shuttle flights. Unhappy people leading less-than-half-happy lives, calculated on a sheer number of weekly hours (preparing + commuting + working) versus number of hours (awake). Yes, values are squishy and personal, but understanding your values in a workplace environment is a vital prerequisite to living on your terms in the time of your life.

What Life Experiences Do I Want to Leverage and Fulfill?

Let's briefly return to this chapter's lead off question: What about the whole you makes you the best at _____? This "whole" is simply the you who has upended the work/life balance and has confirmed IT'S ALL LIFE. It is silly to think that you need to close off major parts of who you have become via your unique collection of experiences for the mere pleasure (or task) of making money. In fact, I would argue that being able to draw on whatever significant life experiences you'd like to incorporate in your everyday adventures is an immense source of power, differentiation, and happiness. If you like speaking a particular foreign language, were involved in some extraordinary event that has changed your perspective, or have been extensively trained in boating safety—**whatever** you'd like to use on a daily basis—these elements should naturally be incorporated into your all-day affairs.

Likewise, you must have dreams about doing certain things: living and working in a foreign country, climbing Mount Kilimanjaro, seeing the world's largest ball of string, and so on. Again, these desires are specific to you and you alone. Understanding what these desires are and incorporating them into your daily life in some way—joining a firm with overseas offices, saving both vacation days and funds for your African adventure, planning your next road trip—is also critically important.

A caveat needs to be addressed at this point. There are a few specific experiences that the Five Ps unfortunately cannot **directly** help you fulfill. Finding a significant other or spouse or bearing kids with him or her are two that immediately spring to mind. These kinds of transformative events cannot be planned with any degree of certainty. It is usually an angelic (or biologic) X-Factor that makes these introductions. This established, if you are passionate about life, if you are in the process of figuring out or executing your mission, the odds of finding or creating that special someone increase dramatically. Birds of a feather **do** flock together, and the laws of attraction clearly state that exuding that positive, happy, and self-confident air resultant of working your passions is a surefire way to have partners come to you. (Hmm... maybe I should join the throng of online dating services.... Has www.MissionMatch.com been taken?)

FINANCIAL ACCOUNTING 101

The tool we will use to flesh out and categorize these topics comes from a financial statement coincidentally used to judge the overall health of a company: the trusty balance sheet. For our purposes, I'd like to call it your "personal balance sheet." If you aren't familiar with how a balance sheet works (or might have forgotten or wanted to forget badly enough), let me give a brief overview of its structure and logic, because this is all you need to know to make this tool perform.

Balance sheets are divided into assets—things that **generate** money, such as cash, property, and equipment—and liabilities, or things that **require** money, such as accounts payable and debt payments. Each section is broken down into short- and long-term categories. Short-term categories (or line items as they are often called) typically relate to things whose value will change within a year; long-term categories consist of everything else. Figure 7.1 highlights these categories.

Personal Balance Sheet

	Assets	Liabilities
Short Term		
Long Term		

FIGURE 7.1 Balance sheet structure.

In creating your personal balance sheet, these categories take on new meaning. **Short-term assets** are skill sets that you are innately great at and love to use—however you want to define them and at whatever level of detail. **Short-term liabilities** are functions that you know you aren't good at or don't enjoy using (although you might be good at them). Let's try to limit the number of short-term entries to, say, five per side. If all you can muster is three, that's fine too. For ease of generation, these short-term entries can be classified into "personal" and "professional" buckets to separate personality and character strengths and weaknesses from those that are more functional in nature. Also, give your releases and meta-passions a gander, because there may be some interesting and useful data there to draw on.

Your long-term assets and liabilities consist of two entries: values and experiences. Asset-side values are those four to five characteristics you want to surround you in a workplace setting. In the other camp, those values you'd like to avoid like the tax man should be banished to the liability column. There are no defining criteria about the kind of words used here—as long as you understand their essences and are comfortable with what you are recording. Referring to the "inspiration" section of your releases might provide some nifty overlaps here, too.

The Second P: Proficiencies

Experiences in your Assets column are any significant events you want to incorporate into your all-day affairs. These can include everything from traveling to life-altering events to a real-life infatuation with fly-fishing. In the Liabilities context, think about the top four or five positive experiences you have always imagined doing but for some reason haven't yet. These could be anything from seeing the Sphinx and Pyramids in Egypt, living in a different city or country, going sky-diving, or running for a particular office. These line items can be likened to high-yield or credit card debt, the kind that costs you upward of 10% to use. You know you want to—in fact, need to!—pay this off, because the longer you wait, the more interest you'll accrue at a pronounced rate. Figure 7.2 provides a clear depiction of both the structure and content of a personal balance sheet.

Assets	Liabilities
Short Term	
Networking	Can't manage up
Analyze trends	Won't say 'No'
Sell a GOOD product	Dislikes confrontation
Travel/hospitality marketing	Bore quickly
Public speaking	Details
Long Term	
Values	
Honesty	Grandstanding/people who talk too much
Following through on commitments	Insensitivity
Being fair and balanced	People colluding behind your back
Experiences	
Working with golf pros	Grow a business
Marketing experience	Work with numbers
Non-profit work	Live and work overseas
Relationships with sports media	Provide for family
	Founder's Stock
	2,288

Figure 7.2   Personal balance sheet example.

THE MOST VALUABLE PART OF ANY BALANCE SHEET

One final long-term liability requires an introduction. As an investor, or perhaps even more appropriately, as the owner of your enterprise, the most valuable part of your balance sheet is what is called founder's stock. **Founder's stock** are the shares you issue to yourself when you start a business. Their initial value on a per-share basis is relatively miniscule, yet their **potential** value can be **astronomical** depending on how you use them. Can you guess what this number represents in the context of your personal balance sheet? It is simply the number of weeks you have left to live using standard actuarial tables, presuming you follow the rules and die on time. Just for fun, let's quickly calculate a decent approximation of your current level of founder's stock:

If you are a man, subtract your current age from 78, multiply by 5, and add a 0 to the end.

If you are a woman, subtract your current age from 84, multiply by 5, and add a 0 to the end.

Currently, you have roughly _____ weeks of founder's stock to use, presuming the bell curve rings true (although those persnickety X-Factored winds have a way of blowing just when you least expect them). Start thinking about all your future plans, conquests of various sorts, vacations, places you've wanted to go, things you want to do—**whatever and however you have imagined your future to be.** Does it look like they will fit? If so, how? You may have heard the question, "If you had all the money in the world, what would you do?" That question is a decent attempt to help focus your time, but it intrudes too much on the Stockdale Paradox—believe you will win, but be real. In the context of your founder's stock, consider this proxy, "You have a decent shot at living _____ more weeks. How do you want to spend that time?"

This version of founder's stock differs in a couple of important ways from that recognized by generally accepted accounting principles. You cannot split, repurchase, reissue, turn into another class of stock, or use them as collateral. Your stockpile will continually deplete, perhaps abruptly or at an accelerated rate. These differences aside, the primary function of your founder's stock is pretty much the same as in a for-profit context: How do you want to use it, leveraging your assets and recognizing your liabilities, to realize your goals?

DATA COLLECTION

Filling out your personal balance sheet might (or might not) take a little time and reflection. Remember, we are looking for only four or five entries per section. I have two suggestions should more entries appear. First, see if you can combine your thoughts in a more holistic term, that is, "pleasing people," "diligent," and "going the extra mile" might be replaceable with "service focused" or "service oriented." Second, trust your gut! If you get uncomfortable with any entry, explore your discomfort and put it to bed on the spot if possible. Also, as you are recording your entries, don't be surprised if a marauding pattern or two jumps out of nowhere and causes you to reflect on how you're allocating your founder's stock. These patterns have been known to start lurking in this part of the process.

Here emerges a splendid opportunity to tap your world for its observations about what you think of yourself. Much like marketing plans require market research, sending your version 1.0 personal balance sheet to a distinct set of acquaintances can be extraordinarily useful. Learning how others from different contexts perceive your assets and liabilities is equally as important for your growth as how you see them. Colleagues from this job or that, a significant other, kids if they are old enough, siblings, parents, or an old school friend can all be helpful in this regard. If your lives have crossed for a good period of time, ask them for their feedback—shades of what you already have or completely new entries. Comparing your perceptions with those of the world around you; distinguishing patterns that may confirm, deny, or augment your initial data; and updating as necessary are vital to the efficacy of this tool.

This might seem a lot like the sometimes-dreaded 360-degree feedback process wherein your fellow workers from all levels encircle and pelt you with their observations. This case differs in that you get to choose who reviews you and your overall standing, and your bonus won't be impacted if you don't "implement the suggested improvements based on your performance results." Most importantly, if you present your questions to the important people in your life in the context of "Hey, I'm trying to improve myself, and I'd really appreciate your input" versus "Oh crap, I've gotta listen to an hour of feedback about what a rotten _____ I am," the process can be quite enjoyable and the additional data invaluable. Intuitively, it is only by identifying what you can passionately be the best at that will make people stop and say, "Wow, you really are the _____ rock star!"

Mirror, Mirror, On the Wall...

After your personal balance sheet is completed, give it a good and thorough review. Look, for example, to see if any of your liabilities (both short term and long term) might explain why you haven't been satisfied, didn't feel you were producing your best, or frankly were passed over or even fired in any of your past working environments. For example, a salient short-term liability displayed in the earlier example is an inability to "manage up," or in a slightly different nuance "deal well with authority." That author doesn't like doing it and isn't good at it, and his abilities to advance in a corporate setting have been repeatedly confounded by it. What does this mean for his future career options? Hhmmm… Maybe the corporate scene is not where he should be focusing his work efforts. Interestingly enough, combining this with his "bores easily" short-term liability and his long-term values liability of disliking "people conspiring behind his back" might additionally discount many such opportunities that come his way. Although these sorts of realizations may be a rude awakening, just knowing **why** certain routes haven't worked and then being able to focus your LifeTime on those that **can** is an immense and powerful relief. (As a note, the character who provided the passion pyramid example from the prior chapter and the personal balance sheet above is now using his MBA in residential real estate.)

Do you see any such themes in your collective entries? Perhaps it an impassioned proclivity for making large teams run smoothly while wanting to work overseas and leveraging a fascination with ships; being a happy worker bee given the right queen and hive combined with the urge to merge your love of surfing into your daily schedule; or the capability to do your own thing as long as you can live in Seattle, spend time with your kids, and travel four weeks a year. You are still in brainstorming mode, so no idea, no matter how "tangential" or "off base," should be discounted or dismissed. Anything come screaming from your scrawlings? If so, write it down!

The other novel feature of this document is its ability to mirror, focus, and augment your work from the prior P. Short- and long-terms assets could very well be reasons (meta-passions) behind your releases or could easily be releases themselves. Taken as a whole, your personal balance sheet is a strong contributor to the understanding and actualizing of your mission. As you did in the last P, look for an overarching explanation, a common net that traps your entries, starting with your long-term experiences from both columns.

Ask yourself, "Why do I want to infuse these particular experiences into my daily cycle, and why do I want to achieve these specific goals before my founder's stock runs out? What about these entries links them all together?"

Next, expand your gaze to the Values section, because your values typically provide a strong indicator and basis of your mission. Put this ball on your mental tee and take a swing. Ask yourself, "What if my values, likes, and dislikes overlaps with the nature of my desired experiences?" It could be something change oriented or status quo extending. It could be something profound or superficial. Above all, though, it should be simple. There is no need for Freudian analysis or cosmic alignment to figure this out.

Finally, look at your short-term assets, because they are the means that will allow you to monetize your mission. "How can I best use my skill sets—what I love to do and am great at—in leveraging my experiences to meet my milestones?" Please don't let anything shy of running out of blood stop you from writing down whatever you are thinking.

At this point, you may want to refer back to the graphic you created in the prior P and try some concepts in the "Mission" triangle on top. Again, your mission is bound to your meta-passions, which simultaneously channel this energy through to your releases. What overarching effort can you define that comfortably sits with your meta-passions and is reflected in your releases to date? Something **really** extraordinary might visibly start coalescing here, and if you sense you are on the verge of something, keep working your words. You have reached the point where simply articulating your mission is the final hurdle. As always, don't worry if you still seem to be stuck in a fog. Keep thinking, stay mellow, and iterate. You have built the structures; your mission will come!

VALERIE: CASE STUDY

Remember the Valerie case study from Chapter 6? She was looking to make some fairly large changes in her life long term and had begun with a diagram of her passion pyramid. She next worked on her personal balance sheet.

Proficiencies

Valerie was able to finish her personal balance sheet rather quickly—in about 25 minutes. A consolidated version follows.

Assets	Liabilities
Short Term	
Networking/communicating	Selling with a quota
Sales/fundraising	Confronting slippery people
Organized/efficient/productive	Leadership skills
Event planning	Creativity
Entrepreneurial	Delegating
	Not giving her all
	Trust too much
Long Term	
Values	
Integrity	Impatient
Sincere/genuine	Wishy-washy/untrustworthy
Relentless/persistent	Unprofessional
Caring	

continues

VALERIE: CASE STUDY (CONTINUED)

Experiences	Marriage
People (friends/family)	Kids
Travel to cool places	Travel to Italy and South America
Living near the ocean	
	Founder's Stock
	~ 2,300

I'd like to note some interesting and perhaps relevant themes in Valerie's personal balance sheet. First off, she loves to sell and can be extremely good at it (a short-term asset); however, she doesn't like the pressure of a quota (a short-term liability). Second, a skill set, event planning, is also one of her releases; this is not uncommon. This is a strong indicator that this strength/passion should be highlighted in her working life. Third, she has many of the classic entrepreneurial skill sets—extremely productive and organized, great with people and developing business, and so on, although she aptly sees a short-term liability as a lack of "leadership skills," specifically being creative and delegating. Compensation issues aside, although this "round-peg-square-hole" situation may curtail any standard start-up, it should not preclude her from exploring franchise opportunities because the beauty of this business-in-a-box model is that someone else has already done the vast majority of the creative planning and process work. Lastly, Valerie exhibits no real liabilities that would necessarily make her nonoptimal in either a corporate or sole proprietor role, as long as she can find an A-grade company to work for.

Passion + Proficiencies = Work Options

Valerie then laid her passion graphic next to her personal balance sheet to see if any nifty work options might materialize. She almost immediately blurted out, "You won't believe this, but I just had a conversation with a good friend from college who just bought a day care center franchise. In fact, I will be seeing him next week. Wow! I would absolutely love to do that, and I know I could do it!" She was amped. Dutifully, though, she kept on going, looking at her inputs and reflecting. Within another five minutes, she had written down the following entries as potential work options now and in the future, depending on her priorities:

- Real estate agent/broker
- Executive role in a nonprofit
- Working for an alma mater
  - Admissions
  - Liaison
  - Major gifts officer
- "Ambassador"
- PR—events, and so on
- Mommy/wife

What's interesting to note here is how these possibilities overlap and can quickly zero in on specific options. For example, marketing for a nonprofit organization is a no-brainer. Valerie quickly rattled off a couple other options in this context: doing PR/event planning for her city, the local Chamber of Commerce, or a nonprofit she is on the board of. The important takeaway is the breadth and overlap of the options she was able to generate. **Your mission and meta-passions don't often change, although your releases easily can to accommodate your shifting priorities.** What is also fascinating, particularly given a long history with large corporations, is that not one such position is mentioned here. To what extent do you think Valerie's prior "success" has been generated by blood, sweat, and tears versus an impassioned core?

I have a final and critical observation. Valerie's last work option (coincidentally?) reflects two of her three experience liabilities: getting married and having kids. Intuitively, these desires should play a part in her search for her new working life. The obvious

continues

> **VALERIE: CASE STUDY (CONTINUED)**
>
> issue becomes where she can spend the most time meeting people who fit a particular demographic and psychographic profile, particularly those who share some of her releases and meta-passions. We will return to this question with more data and focus in the next P.

HOW PROFICIENT ARE YOUR PROFICIENCIES?

You've pestered your work colleagues, kids, neighbors, the postman, and Grandpa Joe about what they think you are good and not-so-good at, and you might have even eyed the dog for his feedback. Take a deep breath, give your shoulders a little massage, and do something you **really** enjoy tonight for completing a task most of us don't even want to start. There might have been more than a few surprises along the data-gathering trail, and you have created something that can serve and guide you for the rest of your life. Congratulations!

Now, document in hand, ask yourself three questions:

- How many of my assets are being levered to the hilt, and how many of my liabilities (experience aside) am I able to avoid like the plague by my current career path? (You might want to circle your answers here.)

  Odds are the number of entries you have circled is not particularly high. Yes, you might have risen to where you are through education, force of will, something you are good at (but don't love), and so on, and these factors can go a long way. However, you probably aren't **really** exploiting what you passionately excel at in your everyday, working affairs. Instinctively, you want to maximize the number of circled assets and liabilities.

■ To what degree does my current career path lend itself to retiring my long-term liabilities?

This question underscores the impossibility of "balancing" work and life and asks you to start aligning what you want from your LifeTime with your work as intimately as possible. An observation here: Sometimes your experience liabilities aren't attainable directly through your work. "Well, I really want to see the Amazon River before I die. However, my mission is being the best retail customer service professional I know. I don't see how my work can take me there, although I do know I need a job that pays me $_____ per year so that I can save enough to go in three years." This mode of thought is completely capiche. Why? Because in some cases you simply need the fruits of your labor to fund the retirement of these liabilities, and this example shows you have done your homework. You know the cost, and you are saving to make it happen. This notion can be extrapolated to paying for junior's summer camp, buying that second home, or whatever else is important enough to you to list as a long-term liability. Again, though, finding work that can directly take down these liabilities probably makes the most sense.

■ What other work options might allow me to better leverage my assets and start knocking off my experience liabilities?

This is where the sizzle really starts kicking in. Look at your entire Assets column and your experience liabilities, and try to imagine a life **and a lifestyle** based on incorporating these entries. Start with what you excel at and love to do. Imagine using your unique talents, skills, values, and experiences to lead a life of your making. Imagine what you'd be wearing, where you'd be working, and whom you'd be interacting with. Imagine the success you'd feel from working your passions and experiencing your liabilities, and imagine that success filling all parts of your life. Feels pretty good, doesn't it? (You might want to write down whatever you are imagining for future reference.)

The more pattern analysis you can apply to answering this question, the more plentiful and "outside your box" your answers will be. This is critical because you might have been locked into—or at minimum constrained—by your experiences in particular functions, industries, and so on. You think because you have been filing people's personal tax returns for seven years or are certified to clean people's teeth that that's all you can do. Hogwash! It might take some doing, sacrifice, and time, but remember that the only thing holding you back from living in the time of your life is you. In fact, realizing and grappling with the sheer number of opportunities that might be available can overwhelm you right from the start. Again, no ideas from this routine should be considered "bad" or "impractical" as of yet!

The final exercise of this P is about to begin. Looking at whatever work choices you have uncovered, refer to your mission outputs thus far and ask yourself, "How can my mission or meta-passions (depending on their relative stage of development) be channeled through any of these potential releases?"

The Second P: Proficiencies

There's nothing binding or overly complex here. It's just a quick screen to assess the degree to which potential work options might have some traction going forward and denote any that appear to meet your criteria.

Onward to P number three!

CHAPTER 8

THE THIRD P: PRIORITIES

WHAT IS MOST IMPORTANT TO YOU, WHERE YOU ARE IN LIFE?

A SLIGHTLY DIFFERENT PERSPECTIVE

Ms. Clarena Tolson currently serves as streets commissioner of the City of Philadelphia, a major public works agency consisting of five divisions: sanitation, highway, traffic engineering, street lighting, and administration. In this position, she oversees more than 2,100 employees with an annual operating budget of $147 million. I had the fortune to see her in a Women in Leadership panel discussion at Wharton, where she had studied.

A major topic was predictably work/life balance. (I promise I kept my mouth shut when the topic was presented in this fashion.) Another Wharton graduate who had recently retired with a small fortune and no kids after a couple of decades in financial services started off and bluntly kyboshed the issue, "There is no way I could have been able to do what I did without giving my work **first** and **sole** focus." There was a palpable note of subdued panic in the room because everyone present probably wouldn't have minded being able to comfortably retire at a relatively young age; this woman's hard-line proscription wasn't what they wanted to hear, though.

Clarena then calmly took the mike, "I'd like to offer a slightly different perspective." Clarena not surprisingly is incredibly hard working and dedicated to both her responsibilities and her reports. I will never forget hearing how she has stayed up to 5 AM, personally cooking a "Thanksgiving" meal in her home for her top 20 colleagues. "I wanted to give personal thanks to them from me for their hard work." She also let it be known that she breast fed each of her three children until they were one. Is she superhuman? An out-of-control, Type A masochist?

Hardly... Clarena embodies a contented, casual, and confident spirit with the discipline of a saint. No airs, no swagger, no attitude. She had a deceptively simple, what-you-see-is-what-you-get persona that responded to the question of "balance" in the following way:

"I quickly realized that focusing on what was most important was the only way I was going to succeed at both raising my kids and doing my job. My husband also is in business, so we didn't have a lot of extra time." She continued, "For example, I hired someone to clean our house since there was simply no way it was going to get done. Another thing I realized [was] that my employees would respect me no matter how I looked. I didn't need to wear the latest fashions or get all spruced up every morning, which can take up a lot of time." It wasn't that Clarena's appearance was anything less than professional or befitting someone in her position—she simply chose not to allocate her time to that particular endeavor. I wanted to give her a standing ovation.

Clarena's perspective boldfaces three key concepts.

1. (AGAIN) LIFE IS NOT A BALANCING ACT

Clarena looks at life not as a series of balances, but priorities. Trying to "balance" everything is intuitively impossible, and the metaphor implies that your respective responsibilities are weights, when in reality they merely have different priorities but are still important and value-adding. Her examples represent tactical manifestations of a much larger and all-encompassing framework that, if you commit to and iterate, can produce leaps in your personal productivity and happiness. This concept is fully explored in a few more paragraphs.

2. YOU DETERMINE THE TERMS OF YOUR PRIORITIES

This is a critical distinction with huge implications. Clarena's reference to her realization that she, not the latest edition of *Working Woman* or some other social or business influence, should decide her appearance at the office is a prime illustration of this notion at work. You should integrate this principle across the entire range of your life and work priorities—how you decide to allocate your personal budget, how long you commute to and from work, how you want to prioritize the time of your life. It is **your** founder's stock, and **you** decide how you want to use it! By far, the largest factor that this concept might impact is your work: where you work, how often you travel and where, compensation, culture, wearing a suit, length of a standard workday, working from home, et cetera. You need to identify, prioritize, **and** actualize all these facets if you desire to create a happy and productive working life.

3. You Can Have "It" All if You Give "It" Your All

This observation has two vital drivers. First is defining what "it" is. Is "it" being able to retire at a certain standard of living by age 50? Being able to travel the world on someone else's dime? Running a mom-and-pop business or a Fortune 500 firm? Carving out a life that prioritizes your kids while making the money needed to afford them the best life can offer? However you define "it," because it's **completely** up to you, if you commit your 110% to the necessary priorities and then focus on making them happen, you can have "it" all!

In fact, from a study supporting their groundbreaking book *Work and Family—Allies or Enemies*, Stewart Friedman and Jeffrey Greenhaus recorded that 55% of men and 43% of women in dual-earner families agreed they could attain the holy grail of having a rewarding career, satisfying family relationships, and having a fulfilling personal life. At its essence, the notion is almost self-fulfilling—you can survive the "how" if you have a "why." Ever wanted something—even something you thought was out of your reach—so badly you would do whatever it took to get it? And (be honest now) if you gave the whatever-it-was your unadulterated, no-holds-barred, no-caveats best effort, what was the result? Most importantly, though, how happy, amped, pumped, and impassioned were you along your volitional way?

The second driver harkens from the Stockdale Paradox. You **must** base what you want in cold, stark reality. For example, do you like to worry about your personal finances? Can't you imagine being suddenly transported into reruns of *Lifestyles of the Rich and Famous*? (And I am not saying this milestone is not possible!) How you deal with and leverage your assets in the process of defining your journey and success is critical in setting these internal expectations. Again, review your personal balance sheet, and ask yourself some potentially tough questions.

For example, perhaps you think, "I am decent, not great, at making teams work, and frankly, I don't really like it." From experience (and I would love to be proved wrong here), you will probably never run a large organization. Likewise, if stability, having a defined function, and cushy benefits are important, small companies or your own company probably won't be optimal. Mind you, there is nothing wrong with these realizations (again, realizing them can be quite liberating) unless your imagined road to success is paved with Big Company W-2s and stock certificates. Deal with it.

I have no idea how Clarena defines what she wants, although a statement she made about being so happy to be able to leave the office at 5 to see her daughter's basketball game provides a little insight. What struck me about Clarena in this context is the distinct impression that her expectations were clearly aligned with her capabilities, and consequently she appeared to be fundamentally happy with life.

SO PASS THE DAYS OF OUR LIVES

Clarena's story also subtly draws out a critical observation of this chapter and perhaps the entire process. As your life changes and evolves, so do your priorities. Think back merely five or ten years. Has what was important to you—how you allocated your LifeTime—changed a little... or perhaps a lot since the hubbub and halcyon of days passed? Have certain elements of life magically appeared, taken on new meaning, whereas others have mysteriously faded away? Although your personality probably hasn't changed a whole lot, the world in which you operate and how you are choosing to interact with that world has more than likely changed dramatically. Intuitively, **as your priorities change, so might the nature of your work need to change to accommodate these new pulls and demands on your LifeTime**. It could be something as simple as working a new schedule, moving to a less demanding function in your workplace, or working from home more often. It could be something as drastic as leaving an industry or function and refocusing your efforts on something completely different. Again, the average American worker changes careers four times during his working life; perhaps unconsciously, you are already doing this.

Understanding your priorities and being able to proactively reassess them as your LifeTime evolves is a powerful and pragmatic tool to have at your disposal. Wouldn't it be great to be able to both plan **and** execute these transitions rather than enduring the duress and frustration of needing to constantly react? You will learn how to establish and review your priorities in a few paragraphs using a process called the prioritization matrix. Then you'll develop the means to tactically execute your priorities utilizing a document development technique called guiding principles.

Before getting into the working mechanisms of these toolsets, I want to drive home the power that a change in priority can have on your working life with a real story of a gentleman named Jim. By far one of the most ground-shaking events that can shift your priorities is having kids. This said, everything is relative: starting a new job, losing an old job, losing a loved one or pet, moving to a new city, or even falling in love—all these events may signal the need to re-examine your priorities and their impact on how you want to allocate your LifeTime.

JIM

Jim was an orphan and an alcoholic. By his recollection, he had been drinking for the majority of his life when his wife had Christopher. He would come home from managing a local hotel, open the fridge, and start drinking whatever-was-in-it until whatever-was-in-it was gone. A 12-pack a night was not an exception. This wasn't the best situation for his wife, who eventually left him, taking Christopher with her. Jim's life continued to spiral downward. He moved into the hotel he was managing but realized he hated the stress of the job.

One night, his son was supposed to visit. Jim was too drunk to deal with him, and this was when he encountered his core. He rightfully observed that no one in the world would or could ever love his son as much as he, and that if he didn't provide this love and financial support, his son would face a similar situation as he did growing up. He stopped drinking two nights later and hasn't gone back since. He left the hotel, slept in his car for a week, and then took a stress-free jack-of-all-trades position in another hotel for eight months, saving his money and making friends with his past. He mended relations with his father, who had been estranged from him for 20 years and even moved back in with him for a spell. Most importantly, he kept in touch with his son and saw him as often as he could.

Now Jim is looking to buy a little place in the area. He realized that he needed a job where he was in more or less total control, so he left his ten years in the hotel business and started a livery service focusing on airport runs. He has a fleet of two Volvo station wagons, each maintained to a tee. He is ALWAYS on time and ALWAYS enthused to greet his passengers. He has been making his alimony payments on time, pays for Christopher's karate lessons, and spoils him as only a father can. One night, he beamingly informed his rides that Christopher had placed first in a state-wide karate contest. You'd have thought he had won the lottery he was so happy. Most importantly, his work allows him to spend a significant amount of time with his son, tons more than he ever could have been able to in his prior working life.

THE PRIORITIZATION MATRIX

The prioritization matrix is a classic consulting tool that quickly and easily allows you to prioritize anything: from which work projects should receive the most attention, to what criteria are the most important to you in a compensation package, to where you want to go on vacation.

The matrix works like this.

First, you must identify all pertinent criteria influencing a particular topic. As an initial example, let's start with something topical—say figuring out how you want to prioritize your LifeTime. Ask yourself, "How would I describe or categorize the different parts of my life that are important to me?" Let's assume you have kids. You might come up with a list consisting of six categories (or buckets, in consultant-speak): work, money, kids, family, friends, and activities. Again, **you** decide how you want to divvy things up. The more granular and personal you can make these determinations, the more powerful and insightful your results will be. I like to call this particular version your **life matrix**.

Next, create a template two columns wider and one column more vertical than the number of categories you have decided upon. Using a spreadsheet for this step also works nicely and can simplify things as this process continues. Fill in the left column and top row with your categories, as in Figure 8.1.

	Work	Money	Kids	Family	Friends	Activities	
Work							
Money							
Kids							
Family							
Friends							
Activities							

FIGURE 8.1   Life matrix worksheet.

Now, moving left to right, top to bottom and ignoring those redundant cells, ask yourself the simple question, "Is the row entry more important than the column entry? That is, is work (what I do) more important than money (how much I make)?" If it is, put a 1 in that square; if it isn't, put a 0. It's a simple, gut-level, binary response: 1 or 0.

Continue:

Is my work more important than my kids?

Is my work more important than my family?

Is my work more important than my friends?

Is money more important than my work?

Is money more important than my kids?

And so on.

Go ahead. Find a pen or pencil and fill in your answers. They're simple decisions of yes or no. Don't waffle, and for your sake, BE HONEST.

Okay. Are you finished? That wasn't so difficult, was it?

Now for the final step: Name the far right column Priority, total your entries from that row, and enter their sums in this column. The higher the score, the more important that factor is to you at the present time. What is great about this tool, aside from its simplicity, is that it gives you **immediate** and **relative** quantitative insight as to what your priorities should be. Why "should be?" Let's look at your answers to the exercise. Your responses and final scores probably look something like Figure 8.2.

	Work	Money	Kids	Family	Friends	Activities	Priority
Work		1	0	0	1	1	3
Money	0		0	0	0	1	1
Kids	1	1		1	1	1	5
Family	1	1	0		1	1	4
Friends	0	1	0	0		1	2
Activities	0	0	0	0	0		0

FIGURE 8.2   Sample completed life matrix worksheet.

If you have kids, they virtually always come out on top; if not, then family usually does. Work typically places in the middle, followed closely by friends and activities. The quest for the almighty dollar typically, if not always, comes in dead last in terms of how you want to be prioritizing the time of your life.

Now, ask yourself the obvious question: How am I spending my ever-depleting, cannot-be-repurchased founder's stock? Habitually, it is being allocated in the exact opposite fashion as how your gut requests it—hence the "should be." What is fascinating about these results is that your gut is probably right on. A study carried out by George Loewenstein asked airport travelers to rank a list of "things that might be important when it comes to making people happy." The list consisted of family life, friends, satisfying work, and a high income (see Table 8.1).

TABLE 8.1   **Rankings and Ratings of Happiness Factors**

Item	Mean Rank	Mean Points
Family life	1.7	37
Friends	2.4	22
Satisfying job	2.5	26
High income	3.6	15

Source: Loewenstein

One was most important, and five was least. Respondents were also asked to assign percentages relating to the importance of each item on the list in its determination of overall happiness.

Stupendously, high income received both the lowest ranking and rating, whereas family life and friends took the top two spots, respectively.

A Metaphored Matrix

A coincidental analogy is at play based on this matrix theme. To start, I will NEVER have half the charisma, acting ability, or sheer gravitas of Laurence Fishburne as Morpheus (or any other role he has played for that matter) in *The Matrix* movie trilogy. I might be able to live up to Keanu Reeves, perhaps, but not Fishburne. In a scene in the first movie, Neo (Reeves) must decide between swallowing a red or blue pill. The blue will return him to a computer-generated version of reality where he can blissfully go on his merry way. The red will allow him to experience the truth.

Metaphorically, I want you to choose the red pill. Obviously, your "reality" is leagues kinder and gentler than the conditions humans faced after being exposed to "the truth" in the movie series. The parallels abound, though: People merely go about their daily business in a fabricated, rules-based environment, emotionless pawns in a game they can never win. Fighting this system ultimately required Neo and others to believe in themselves (their cores) that no matter what, they would prevail. After Neo realized that all he was fighting was code written by others that did not apply to him, he started to win. If I can move you to merely contemplate accepting X-Factors, the fact that you don't "meow," believing in your core, and even peripherally using the Five Ps, **we** are starting to win.

Working the Prioritization Matrix

Let's use the prioritization matrix to beat another dilemma—narrowing in on finding your life's work. Again, the first and most important step is figuring out all the categories that are important to **you**. You might consider the following as a basis from which to start this "new work" matrix, using the same question: "Is _____ more important to me than _____?" per the earlier instructions.

Industry—Your desire to work in a particular industry.

Commuting more than ___ minutes each way—Time required, means, and cost of transport. (You may want to include at least two of these—one for say 30 minutes and another for 60.)

Working in _____ —The geographic location of your work.

Values—The extent to which your values will blossom.

Compensation—Total potential take-home in various forms of wealth.

Mentor—Within the firm; this person can be quite valuable as your career progresses.

Having a great boss—The highest correlating factor in Hadley's "Why I Love My Work" study, regardless of industry, level, or position, is having a good relationship with your direct superior.

Ability to work from home __ days/week—Reduce commute time and costs while increasing productivity.

Big name—Brand recognition and power.

Dress up/dress down—This factor could be important to you.

Feels right—The power of trusting your gut!

Of course, you might want to include many more personal drivers in your new work matrix. Or perhaps the majority of the ones just listed are moot for a variety of reasons. The key thing here is proactively fleshing out these details to establish the parameters for your search. **It is tremendously easier getting what you want if you know what you want.** Once established, any and all work opportunities can be easily screened using these outputs.

Using the matrix to drive new working life options can yield another major benefit: the significant and immediate **reduction** in the number of available options because, in fact, there are **too** many out there to choose from. **The more specific your desires, the easier the process becomes**. For example, let's say you absolutely love where you live. It comes up with the highest score in your matrix, and it would take multiple acts of multiple gods to move you. Yet, you realize, again per your matrix results, you don't want to spend more than 20 minutes commuting to work. The next step is to get out a local map and start drawing circles from your location, establishing the geographic territory where **your** terms will **allow** you to work. This is akin to, in real estate terms, your farming territory—where your focus and knowledge of "what is going on" should be directed. If you can't find work or an employer that pays you what you absolutely need to make, your options are again quite clear. Because location was more important than commute, reduce your costs or figure out a way to make ends meet on your own. Although this may sound risky and downright foolhardy, you might be amazed by the degree of uncertainty you can overcome to live on your terms.

Here's a final context for using matrix results to assess your work opportunities. Imagine being in an interview and being able to discuss precisely what is important to you. Do you think the interviewer will be impressed? Do you think your self-awareness and the ability to quickly cut through to key points would give you a leg up over the competition? People like to deal and work with people who know what they want.

This maxim of getting what-you-know-you-want can be applied to many more topics in life than merely looking for work: where you want to live, the kind of car you need to drive, naming your kids, what you want out of life (experience liabilities!), and so on. The prioritization matrix gives you focus which, in your multi-multi-tasking, pop-up ad, and decision-by-committee way of life, is sorely needed. It is **only** by focusing your LifeTime on **specific** tasks that anything extraordinary will happen, and I believe you want to do something extraordinary at some point (or at many points) in your LifeTime! I will return to this concept of focus driving success a little later in this chapter.

MATRIX THIS!

In the context of "getting by knowing," you should strongly consider running another matrix exploring compensation because this information can be extremely valuable in figuring out two key inputs to your overall plan. First, it can quickly help you narrow the field of potential industries and functions. Put another way, it can help you assess your risk tolerance with respect to different kinds of income. Do you prefer a higher salary with a relatively smaller bonus? If so, sales might not be for you, but a line job might. How willing are you to sacrifice a lower salary in lieu of profit-sharing? If that appeals to you, you might be a good fit for a smaller company. To what extent do you prefer the responsibility of generating your own income? If that desire is high, running your own shop or being a sales agent might satisfy you. Your answers to such questions might surprise you, because these outputs may differ from your current or desired line of work.

The second reason is that these understandings can be tremendously helpful in establishing and negotiating key details of your overall compensation plan. If, for example, you have hooligans with special needs at home, a top-tier insurance plan might be essential. You might give vacation and the ability to work from home a high ranking, or you might not. After you realize where your priorities sit, the process of screening potential options or working with your future boss or hiring manager to figure out ways to meet your needs becomes a whole lot easier. You might be surprised by the degree of flexibility and creativity that exists in getting you to sign on, again presuming you know what is important to you and can focus on those top two or three factors. (Remember the rule of 85%: If you can secure 85% of what you want, the deal should be done.) For example, reviewing her options during a job search a few years back, a good friend successfully negotiated reducing her salary by one week, spread out over the year, in exchange for another week of vacation, while still linking her potential bonus to her original salary level. She ended up not taking the job for other reasons; however, having this term in writing was a big factor in her consideration of dedicating her LifeTime to that particular employer.

WHAT VERSION ARE YOU ON?

Changes in your life inevitably cause you to recalculate your matrices. Your father falls sick, and you realize you want to spend more time with him. Your work takes you to a new city. You get laid off. You get married. You get divorced. You have kids. You want to return them. You figure out what your mission is and decide to move to a new city and enter a new line of work. Whatever… An immensely useful feature of the prioritization matrix is the fact that it can be easily adapted and updated to fit any new life scenario or X-Factor that comes your way.

Most evolutions probably won't cause a big rejiggering of your results. Some will, though, and it is these changes you simply cannot afford your founder's stock to miss.

A BLATANT SECRET

I would like to share a blatant secret as a segue to the "guiding principles" part of this chapter. This secret has assisted those who use it to achieve extraordinary results, milestones they never knew they could meet in their LifeTime. What's their secret? They write down their goals and then plaster them in high eye-traffic locations. "What sort of malarkey is this?" you say. "People can break through their own boundaries and exceed their expectations by merely writing down their goals?" Yes, they can, and you can, too. However, this relatively simple process can be extraordinarily difficult for four potentially overlapping reasons.

The first is dealing with your intrinsic laziness. Admit it. The second is simply not knowing what your goals **should** or **could** be, which can be problematic. The third is an extrapolation of the second—without discrete goals, generating a tactical plan to achieve them is conceptually impossible (and without a plan, you are living on someone else's terms!). Last and perhaps largest, it is difficult, often painfully so, to commit yourself to self-imposed targets that stare you black and white in the face—"expectation fright." Part of this hesitancy might be a fear of success, part might be not knowing how to actualize them, part could be simply not wanting to commit to something that you aren't innately passionate about. Regardless, being objectively accountable to and with yourself is arguably one of the most difficult feats you can pull off. It is so much easier to avoid the whole topic or just say, "Yeah, I have goals," yet not commit them to paper and in the process, not commit yourself to meeting them. The guiding principles process can help you understand and create goals based on priorities that you can comfortably execute.

LET'S MAKE A DEAL!

Ever wonder how all those big deals you read about in the *Wall Street Journal* or *USA Today* happen? Bank of America merges with Fleet Bank. AOL acquires Time Warner; Time Warner would like to divest AOL. IBM teams up with SAP to provide IBM SAP. Bill Gates acquires the Nation of Tahiti for his stock dividend payment. No matter how big or small, power-laden, ego-driven, strategically brilliant, or foolhardy the transaction, chances are at some point a document much like a guiding principles document was created. Yes, two bigwigs must have at some point sat down over poached salmon and Chardonnay and given each other peeks inside their respective kimonos. After they had sized each other up and decided to explore something more personal, the process would typically move to the guiding principles stage, where many deals are either solidified or dissolved.

Guiding principles are high-level terms, each associated with an action plan and milestones, which basically carve up a huge enchilada into bite-sized morsels that you, the implementer, can swallow. Using this format can be extremely fruitful in producing results, particularly in conjunction with your matrix outputs. Let's develop a set of guiding principles based on the outcome of your life matrix, focusing solely on the top three or four ranked categories. (Ever try learning to play golf or snow skiing? How many different suggestions could you implement simultaneously?) Conceptually, your matrix results should feed your guiding principles, like Figure 8.3 shows.

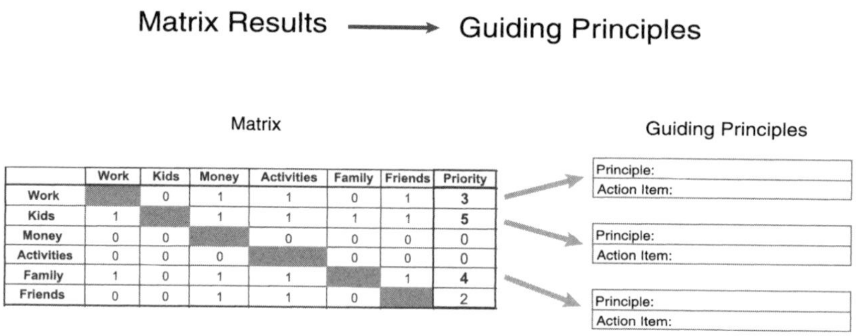

Matrix Results ⟶ Guiding Principles

Matrix

	Work	Kids	Money	Activities	Family	Friends	Priority
Work		0	1	1	0	1	3
Kids	1		1	1	1	1	5
Money	0	0		0	0	0	0
Activities	0	0	0		0	0	0
Family	1	0	1	1		1	4
Friends	0	0	1	1	0		2

Guiding Principles

Principle:
Action Item:

Principle:
Action Item:

Principle:
Action Item:

FIGURE 8.3   Guiding principles.

For the sake of example, let's assume that your top three entries per your initial prioritization matrix were family, work, and money, in that order. Now comes the fun part: Ask yourself three questions per principle:

- What changes do I need to make, **scope of change being irrelevant**, to improve my relationship with this principle? (Remember: You can always run a quick matrix to figure out what is most important here.)

- How do I go about making these changes? (What is the process I must start and finish?)

- What kind of time frame do I need to actualize these changes? (By next week, next month, next year?)

The answer to the first question is the essence of the principle, the content describing what is to happen. The second and third responses combine to form the action plan and milestones you need to undertake to fulfill your principle on time. Your process should be fairly detailed, and milestones for implementation must be realistic and obvious.

Here's an example on the lower end of the seismic change scale:

Principle #1: Family—My family lives all over the map, and I don't interact with them enough.

Action Plan/Milestones—Starting this week, I will set aside an hour per week in my daily planner or software scheduling program to call them.

Principle #2: Work—I am tired of wasting two hours per day commuting. I'd like to be able to work from home one or more days per week.

Action Plan/Milestones

1. I will generate a cost/benefit plan and schedule a meeting with my boss to walk her through my rationale, both within the next week.

2. This weekend, I will research the costs of purchasing and installing all required equipment as part of this plan and will be prepared to incur the costs to be able to actualize this principle.

3. Over the next week, I will research and think about additional ways my boss can judge my performance and will include them in my plan.

Principle #3: Health—I need to eat better and eat out less!

Action Plan/Milestones:

1. Starting this weekend, I will generate a weekly meal plan with enough time to do a grocery run by Sunday night.

2. I will consult my favorite cookbook for easy recipes.

Here's another example that might topple unreinforced buildings:

Principle #1: Family—My father recently died, and my mom is sick. I want to move to be nearer to her.

Action Plan/Milestones

1. Share my thoughts with her today and ask her if I can stay with her until I can get settled.
2. Develop a moving budget by next Monday and estimate how long I can go without income to make the move.
3. Start exploring housing options near her immediately.

Principle #2: Work—I need to explore working off-site with my boss and potentially look for a new job near my mom.

Action Plan/Milestones

1. Notify my boss of my intentions on Monday and see if he's open to keeping me on remotely.
2. Contact any active networks in her area and start working them immediately.
3. Schedule a trip for informational interviews in two weeks.
4. Explore online boards immediately.
5. Ask my mom and her network of friends for help.

Principle #3: Health—My mom has skin cancer. I want to understand how it works, what the potential treatments are, and how it can be prevented.

Action Plan/Milestones

1. Schedule a meeting by next Wednesday with my primary care physician or an internal medicine/oncologist to discuss the topic.

2. Research online by next Friday.

3. Contact my mom's physician and meet with them by next Friday.

This larger-scale example underscore three key takeaways from this P:

- **One priority, many implications**—It is not uncommon for your most important priority to significantly impact and drive your overall set of guiding principles. The budget/need for cash to make the move referenced in the second step of the family Action Plan/Milestones wouldn't need to happen at all if it weren't for your top-line priority.

- **Focus on the big things**—Ever draw up a list of things that you **must** get done today? How often are you able to cross **everything** off that list? My personal results run in the sub-10% range. Why? For openers, you simply try to do too many things. You constantly push yourself to do more and be better at it. Business seems to reward it. Society demands it. Schools teach it. Technology enables it. Software might help with it (then again). Marketing campaigns are built on it... and, from my perspective, there is nothing particularly wrong with it. The key thing that usually makes this process collapse, or at least become tedious, is difficulties in the process of setting and reviewing your expectations, most importantly those relating to your personal performance. How often do you get worked out of shape, stress, freeze, become frustrated, and worst of all **worry** if you can't get **every little last thing** done? Don't sweat it. Focus on the big

---

things, because if you can conquer them, the importance of little things implicitly stays little. Remember the rule of 85%!!

- **The time is now!**—The more time you have to realize and focus on the **infinite** list of "what ifs" surrounding your plans, no matter how large or small, the longer it will take you to actualize and potentially monetize them. One CEO of a software firm was so adamant about making decisions that if you were given a decision and didn't make it within a specific time frame, you would be **axed**. Although this may seem a bit extreme, he would rather his employees make decisions, see what happens, and then iterate them through to success, rather than wasting time essentially prolonging the process.

Note: This is not to say you should up and do whatever pops into your mind at random moments. One of the most important lessons to getting things done is knowing where and how to allocate your LifeTime. After you have developed (and gut-checked) a list of prioritized principles, action plans, and milestones, attack them with the ferocity of a throng of children swarming a piñata carcass.

VALERIE: CASE STUDY

Priorities

Valerie was really getting the hang of these exercises. She was able to generate her key categories and finish three matrices—life, working life, and compensation—in less than 20 minutes. Granted, they could always be more detailed, but for her purposes, they sufficed nicely. They are shown in Figures 8.4 through 8.6.

Life Matrix						
	Family	Friends	Volunteering	Work	Money	Priority
Family		1	1	1	1	4
Friends	0		1	1	1	3
Volunteering	0	0		1	1	2
Work	0	0	0		1	1
Money	0	0	0	0		0

FIGURE 8.4 Valerie's Life Matrix.

No surprises here…

Working Life Matrix						
	Commute	Boss/Mentor	Office Space	Culture	Compensation	Priority
< 30 min.Commute		0	0	0	0	0
Boss/Mentor	1		1	1	0	3
Office Space	1	0		0	0	1
Culture	0	0	1		0	1
Compensation	1	1	1	1		4

FIGURE 8.5 Valerie's Working Life Matrix.

Obviously, Valerie is concerned about her financial picture, particularly paying for her nice townhouse. This said, her focus on a good boss/mentor is smart, although her disregard for spending time on the road is a bit frustrating. I mean, imagine all the face time she could be spending with potential suitors, per her long-term experience liabilities (marriage and kids) not spent on the road.

Compensation Matrix							
	Base Salary	Options	Bonus	Commission	Benefits	Work From Home	Vacation	Priority
High Salary		1	1	1	1	1	1	6
Options	0	0	0	0	0	0	0	0
Decent Bonus	0	1		1	0	1	1	4
Commissions	0	0	0		0	0	0	0
Benefits	0	1	1	1		1	1	5
Work From Home	0	1	0	1	0		1	3
Vacation	0	1	0	1	0	0		2

FIGURE 8.6 Valerie's Compensation Matrix.

continues

VALERIE: CASE STUDY (CONTINUED)

This is Valerie's "best case" compensation scheme. I like all the facets she included here as part of compensation, by the way. This data is telling of a couple key directions that her working life search should take her, which narrow her field immensely. Her desire for a high base salary, no options, a strong benefits package, and a decent bonus all point toward a mature, established company. Likewise, her lack of interest in commissions should direct her away from sales. Her medium interest in working from home provides another nice screen because her focus should be on more progressive industries and employers—software, services, research, healthcare, and so on—and slightly absolves her of her commute infatuation from her working life matrix.

What is also useful about this information is noting where it presently overlaps and doesn't, when matched up against Valerie's potential work option list. Obviously, many of the options on her list (most nonprofit positions, alumni, PR for the Chamber, and so on) cannot support this best-case scenario. Real estate won't either, unless she can do it on the side and build up a client base and reputation that will provide her with the comfort to wean her off the guaranteed salary/bonus structure. The same observation applies to the childcare franchise opportunity.

Here's another question going back to Valerie's long-term experience liabilities and work options: What do you think her odds are of finding a husband/potential father in a corporate setting? She could very well meet someone who could provide her with a lifestyle she prefers, although finding someone who shares in her passions and outlook on life may be difficult. This is a potential issue whose trivial or nontrivial nature only time will tell.

What is important to underscore here is how all three of these matrices will change over time. Let's assume Valerie finds her rich mate and has kids. All three of these outputs will undergo dramatic transformations, and in the process, work options that may have been impractical in the past can now spring to life. Again, a nice aspect of this process is that she has already defined what gets her passion jets firing, and in fact, regardless of future matrimonial designs, she can start planning toward making one or two of these work options real. She can save money, go to classes on the side, research franchises, whatever—knowing what she wants is obviously the critical piece in getting it.

YOUR NICHE

This is where it all comes together. All your work thus far has been done to give you the essential elements of your niche, a domain that you and only you can define and own. In a consumer context, **niches** or **niche markets** are populations that can be segmented and understood with extremely revealing levels of detail and depth. A good example might be female Harley Davidson attire. In the grand scheme of the apparel industry, this is a small market. However, significant information on this market's buying habits, likes and dislikes, and so on can be readily researched, and its overall profitability could be quite compelling.

Breaking into a preexisting niche—one already defined and occupied by your competition—can be expensive, exhausting, and risky; you are implicitly starting the process dealing with a landscape created by someone else's terms. This doesn't mean you can't establish your own and broach the niche your own way with a novel set of offerings—again, it is merely a bit riskier and can require more investment. The flipsides of following are that you can learn from your predecessors' mistakes, and a market has already been established.

A common marketing practice used to get around this issue is simply creating your own niche and positioning yourself as its leader, rather than having to compete with the rest of the world, on their terms. **This is precisely what you have done.** You have defined a market of your making, whose unique passions, proficiencies, and priorities are yours and yours alone. You **already** lead your niche, even if it is just a mere twinkling in your imaginative eye. But first you must properly plan and fund your excursion.

A real-life example of a niche comes from a discussion with a woman who was afraid to go after hers because she thought it wasn't sturdy enough to withstand potential competition. The interchange went something like the following:

> Me: "So, Deb, let me get this straight. Your mission in life is to assist people with a particular condition and their families by starting a novel nonprofit that will establish centers to provide education and training in key hospitals around the country?"
>
> Deb: "Yes. That's right. But I know there are so many other people out there already working in this field. I just don't think I can differentiate myself enough from them in the eyes of donors and decision makers in the hospitals."
>
> Me, reading from her personal balance sheet: "What you are saying is that everyone else out there has the same mission and model, is outgoing, optimistic, an excellent networker and entrepreneurial, wants to incorporate insights from a background in finance and a personal connection with this condition in her daily affairs, has a strong network of banking friends as potential donors, loves to travel, and is fine for the foreseeable future with a nonprofit compensation plan?"

Deb: "Aha. I understand. Gotcha!"

Essentially, you are your niche.

Take the outputs from your first three Ps, print them if necessary, and simply lay them out in front of you. This, in business, is called a **visioning session**. Your new working life is really starting to take shape: what you are passionate about and possibly your mission, what you are innately good at and love to do, both past and future experiences you want to exploit, and what is important to you in life. It is all there, in front of you, looking for a home that **only** you can build and master. Paste these outputs to a wall, on a large sticky pad, or mount them above your bed. Get lost in their patterns and intersections, their unique nuances, their impassioned yearnings, their hidden missives, and most of all, their extraordinary and probably untapped power to create a LifeTime that you define and rule.

This is one of those points in the process where realizations **will** need to be incorporated back into the process and the process itself spun a couple more times. Missions can become obvious, working options lucid, bottled-up decisions can explode or lose their fizz, and priorities of all kinds can be thrown for loops. Imagine living in your niche, down to the smallest possible detail of whatever priority that springs on your mind. This is **your** box— think **inside** it!

Hire a stenographer, find a voice recorder, dull your pen points, but get this stuff down!

TIME TO DEFINE

You have reached the last exercise of this chapter, which is coincidentally the most important assignment in the entire process.

"Assignment" might be the wrong term here, because it rings of having to work through those Algebra 2 problem sets in high school. This step is absolutely critical to the process's success; the term "assignment" is being used solely to convey this seriousness.

Life is the journey, and your journey should drive the way you define your successes, **not** the other way around. Look at your niche documents and ask yourself two simple questions:

#1: "How Do I Define 'Wealth'?"

How **do** you define wealth? Is it a magic number (and if so, has this number gotten larger with LifeTime)? Is it solely something financial, or does it include other priorities, experience liabilities, or a general set of experiences? Does it necessarily require a numerical component? Is it a lifestyle, a mindset, both, or neither? As usual, you control these critical distinctions, and more importantly, their implications. To what extent does your definition "fit" with your passion outputs, personal balance sheet, and priorities? Does it nestle up nicely or poorly protrude? If the latter, what needs to change?

#2: "How Do I Define 'Success'?"

This question shares the same vein, although with a slightly larger needle. Given how you just defined your stick of honey, what does its wrapper look like? Referring to your life matrix results ("what is important to me in life?") and your experience liabilities can be good places to start. Intuitively, looking to your mission and meta-passions for inspiration similarly makes sense. Your description could be a metric or numerical target, for example,

The Third P: Priorities

"Success to me is improving the lives of 10,000 people," "educating 5,000 students," or "providing legendary work for 50 people." It could be something philosophical—that is, "Success to me is living on my terms" or very practical—"Success is raising happy kids." Again, is it a lifestyle, a mindset, both, or neither? Whatever you are thinking, write it down! Bullet points, preambles, whatever... The absolutely vital thing is simply getting your thoughts on paper as you might consider joining those rarified and masochistic few who write down their goals and then execute them with the principle of action plans.

Instinctively, your niche and its elements should blend with and support the way you define your particular flavors of wealth and success like a robust Zinfandel typically needs a good dose of Cabernet to make its nose and essence come alive. The way you define wealth and success is completely up to you and may very well change with your LifeTime. There's nothing wrong with this, and in fact, it's probably a good and **necessary** transition. Conceptually, defining these two fundamental drivers of your personal expectations and happiness is just plain necessary in aligning (or realigning) your LifeTime with your reality. To these ends, you might want to revision your niche once more with these definitions in the mix, per Figure 8.7. (The circular arrows mean "iterate.")

Aspects of your definitions might fly in the face of many "socially accepted" conventions or peer group attitudes about the meaning of LifeTime. There is no better way to ground your forward direction than by possessing a salient understanding of **what**, at the end of a heartbeat, is important to you and **how** you should go about getting it.

Passion + Proficiencies + Priorities = Working Life Options: Your Niche

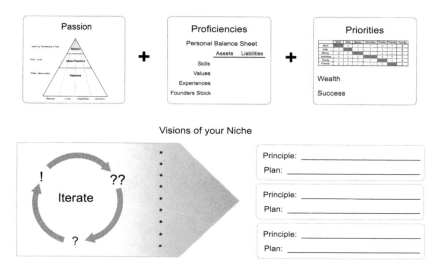

Visions of your Niche

well change with your LifeTime. There's nothing wrong with this, and in fact, it's probably a good and **necessary** transition. Conceptually, defining these two fundamental drivers of your personal expectations and happiness is just plain necessary in aligning (or realigning) your LifeTime with your reality. To these ends, you might want to revision your niche once more with these definitions in the mix, per Figure 8.7. (The circular arrows mean "iterate.")

Aspects of your definitions might fly in the face of many "socially accepted" conventions or peer group attitudes about the meaning of LifeTime. There is no better way to ground your forward direction than by possessing a salient understanding of **what**, at the end of a heartbeat, is important to you and **how** you should go about getting it.

Figure 8.7   Niche visioning layout and process.

The stage has been set for the next P, where we will crystallize your plan to rule your niche. Curtains please!

CHAPTER 9

THE FOURTH P: PLAN

HOW DO YOU BRING YOURSELF TO MARKET?

Let's review. You have an idea of your mission. You know what skills, values, and experiences you want to leverage to claim your niche. You know what life experiences you want to enjoy, at least until you have fulfilled them and have room for more. You know what is important to you in life and have drafted guiding principles with distinct action plans to achieve them. You have decided to take control of how your founder's stock is being allocated. Finally, you have been able to imagine even brief and interrupted snapshots of your impassioned life. **Congratulations**! You have finished the vast majority of your market research. Now comes the **easy** part—sharing this "new you" with the world, your family, your friends, and most importantly, yourself.

From a business perspective, this effort is much like reintroducing a refreshed product or service to new markets. The main difference is that the product or service being rebranded, repositioned, and relaunched is you! Don't worry if these terms are foreign, frightening, or fishy to you. It is merely business-speak for saying to the world, "**Hey, I've got something new and different I think you are going to love. I want to tell you about it, and if you like it, try it out!**" It doesn't matter if Microsoft is introducing a full suite of its latest crash-proof consumer offerings to the pre-K market, General Foods is launching jungle-shaped Dora the Explorer Fruit Loops, or Ford is pioneering a new line of engines that run on cow dung to service the needs of developing markets (and certain parts of Wisconsin and Texas)—they all follow a similar process. Although their bureaucracies might have a bit more money to fiddle with, and their ad and marketing campaigns undoubtedly will be able to put you to sleep, there is actually little difference (internal politics aside) in what they need to do and your next steps. So let's get stepping!

Essentially, making this "relaunch" happen is a three-step process.

1. **Write it down**—First, you must codify certain aspects of your niche with adequate clarity so that even a random layperson can quickly understand a) what you are bringing to your markets and b) how this "new organic you" is different and better-suited for your markets than the preprocessed version. Implicit in this step are further realizations and content refinements resultant of once again iterating your thoughts. From experience, a notable and common realization is the desire to shift your focus from certain communities to markets that matter more in the fulfillment of your mission.

   What is absolutely critical (and enjoyable!) to note is how the "new you" that will emerge from this process is starkly more focused than any prior manifestation. Your perfect "release" might not be readily apparent, and your mission might still need some guidance—your plan need not be ready for prize-winning review. The fact that you have done your research and have defined wealth and success in your terms will forever illuminate your self-perception (and probably public perceptions, too) with a unique spotlight going forward. It is this difference that this plan must capture; the effectiveness of any launch is driven completely by the **self-realization** of the strength of the new product's attributes.

2. **Sell it**—Making successful long-term change requires two additional critical elements: buy-in from key stakeholders, those around you who have a vested interest in seeing you happily working your passions; and investment, or access to investment of various shapes and sizes from a variety of sources.

3. **Execute**—This is possible with the support of key stakeholders and the confidence of a tested plan, which accurately and honestly reflects your niche and the milestones you need to meet in its fulfillment.

    Two pieces of collateral need to be produced to these ends. This P will focus on the first, which is typically only a two- or three-page document, the majority of whose content has **already** been generated and can be reused in the second piece, the topic of the next and final P. (I am here for you!) What sort of cure-all format is this?

THE EXECUTIVE SUMMARY

Ever had the experience of drafting an Executive Summary? It can be incredibly enjoyable and juice-pumping. It can be like trying to pin a greasy pig in a pit of Jello, drunk, with one hand tied behind your back. You can bang out an Executive Summary in three of four hours; you can endure sleepless nights for weeks. It can tear teams apart like an expanding star or solidify them with the pull of a black hole. It's similar to writing a term paper or thesis, in that they often reflect the culmination of your experiences, your thought and reasoning, and hopefully your gut. The most successful ones, not surprisingly, are also written with a large degree of passion.

Executive Summaries are never fully finished either. The competitive landscape can quickly change, people can join and leave the team, and access to funds can curtail or accelerate certain functions. Regardless of what you are proposing—a new product or service offering, a business unit, a company, or an impassioned you—the most exciting and perhaps novel aspect of this process is the fact that you are in the driver's seat, you are in control of the direction of this venture (or adventure as the case might be!). I have been involved with at least ten such forays to date, and looking back, I sorely wish I had directed merely five percent of the LifeTime spent on them creating one for myself. Live and learn, and then live some more and learn some more. Life is an iterative process.

The following structure, headings (which have been stripped of most of their Brooks Brother's business-ese attire), and their associated content have been used successfully in generating the internal consensus and external investment required to bring plans to life.

Mission Statement: What is the mission of this initiative?

What Is Enabling This Venture? Typically, the convergence of three or four disparate trends creates the demand for this opportunity. These trends can include new technologies, shifting demographics, a change in governmental policy, unmet or projected customer requirements, and so on. An excellent example comes from the network equipment explosion that was running rampant at the end of the previous decade. Enabling trends included the introduction of more powerful processors, deregulation of the telephone monopoly, and a projected volcano of data traffic. Combined, their movements created literally hundreds of companies producing traffic routing technologies to capitalize on this demand.

What Will the Company Do? Will it manufacture products or provide services? Will it address the needs of businesses or consumers?

How Will the Company Make Money? Will there be a service component to a product sale? How can you continue to generate revenue from the same customer? Might people want to subscribe for this service or product?

Why You Will Win/What Makes This Company Different? What about this venture's human, physical, or intellectual assets gives you an ongoing step up against whatever competitive forces might enter your market? What about your idea is defensibly different from what exists in the marketplace today and tomorrow?

How Will the Company Market Itself? What is the tagline of the venture? Who is the target market? Where and how will the company and its offerings be positioned? What kind of marketing devices will be deployed to deliver the desired results?

Partnering Requirements: What sort of partnerships does this venture need to forge to be successful? How might your company need to include other organizations in the development, production, marketing, distribution, or servicing of its offerings to enable it to win?

Management: What makes those involved qualified to lead this venture? How credible and relevant are their personal and business backgrounds to the demands of the venture?

Board of Advisors: Whose experiences, knowledge, and relationships can you draw on?

Financial Projections: Include monthly, quarterly, and/or yearly forecasts of revenues, costs, and potential earnings. There is usually an attached spreadsheet that drills down into all aspects of your projections. Financial targets—retiring liabilities, accumulating savings, and so on—are also sometimes included.

Key Success Factors: What three or four absolutely critical things need to happen to enable this company to get out there and start making waves?

Milestones: These are the target dates of completion of a variety of key functions, including making sales and hiring.

Required Investment: How much money do you need, and where will this money come from (investment, sales, and so on)?

Exit Strategy: How and when will investors be able to get paid for their investment, typically through a merger or an initial public offering of stock (IPO)?

Note: If your niche involves setting up your own business, you might want to use this format to present it, along with the subsequent version for selling purposes. This can be a critical part of the overall deliverable and success of this P.

The key thing this document should convey is credibility. Every category listed here—or more specifically, **how** every category listed here is addressed—will confirm or question both the author's and venture's credibility. Why is credibility so important? Simply put, credibility placates risk, and no investor worth his or her fund's salt likes to invest in ventures that have inordinate amounts of risk. Exhibiting an understanding of both your targeted niche and the process and requirements of going after it is absolutely critical. Credibility is the currency that new enterprises trade with. Credible risk + opportunity for high returns = $$.

YOUR VERSION: THE LIFE SUMMARY

You can apply every one of these headings to how you will tactically relaunch an impassioned you, albeit with slightly different content. Your version—what I will call your Life Summary—will serve you like a AAA trip planner. It will provide you with miles between milestones, a thorough list of things you should bring, a travel budget calculator, emergency numbers, and most importantly, a description of your end destination. Again, don't fret if all this is new to you. Let me walk you through your version, explore and explain differences in the content, and refer to where most of this data might already be patiently and anxiously waiting. Some entries are fairly self-explanatory, whereas others will require more detail. Are you ready?

Mission Statement: What is your mission? What do you want your tombstone to say? **Passions: mission statement**

What Is Enabling Your Venture? What overarching trends—both work and life—do you see "coincidentally" converging that both enable and drive your change? One way to think of these trends is to reflect on the notion, "I have reached the point in my life where I realize _____ is important to me, and I need to make a change." These realizations can range as far as your eye can see:

- **Geography**—"I am sick of living in the city. I need to get out."
- **Work**—"I realize I no longer want to commute so far to work. I need something I can do that is much closer or preferably that I can do out of the house."
- **Relationship**—"I realize I am not happy with my current relationship. I need to get out and leave the whole mess behind me."
- **Opportunity**—"My skill sets could be applicable in this different industry that gets my passion fires raging. I need to switch employers." Or, like Julie Aigner-Clark, founder of Baby Einstein, the infant toy company, might have said to herself, "I heard about this study coming out that shows that kids who listen to Mozart learn better. How can I leverage this to meet my mission?"
- **Et cetera**—You know the way your waters flow better than anyone else!

Passion at Work

These trends should reflect what is important to you and what you'd like to leverage in the process of satisfying your unmet needs. In this context, reviewing your top three results from your prioritization matrix work can yield relevant and valuable information. **Priorities: matrix results**

What Will You Do? How do you define wealth and success, and how do you want to focus your LifeTime in meeting these definitions? Through a start-up or the government? A nonprofit or a Fortune 1000 firm? Through your own efforts? Or as a stay-at-home father or mother, for the time being, until the kids are older and you'd like to return to _____? **Priorities: matrix results, definitions, and niche visioning results**

How Will You Make Money? What is important to you in your overall compensation package, given your current priorities? This can include everything from a certain salary/bonus/commission structure to the number of vacation days you'd like, the length of your commute, flex hours, working from home, and so on. Although this might seem like an odd place to mention this content, remember that time is **both** money **and** life. **Proficiencies: Asset side of your personal balance sheet; Priorities: compensation matrix results and niche visioning results**

Why You Will Win/What Makes the "New You" Different? Fundamentally, what sets you and your niche apart from those of the hordes of other future beach-bound retirees? What assets and experience liabilities do you have that give you an unbeatable step up in carving out and defending your niche? **Proficiencies: short- and long-term assets and experience liabilities of your personal balance sheet**

How Will You Market Yourself? I'd like to focus on one particular and essential component of any standard marketing plan—branding. What is a brand? It is simply whatever attributes you consciously or unconsciously associate with **any** interaction with an entity: name, logo, font/color schemes, tag lines, product or service characteristics, sounds, employees, and so on. What do you think of when you hear the word "Volvo"? (Safety?) Starbucks? (Sophisticated and delicious consumables?) Victoria's Secret? (Classy lingerie and clothes?) Funny enough, people will gladly spend a small fortune to buy the best brand they can (or can't) afford. By one mode of thought, the value of a brand is a company's market value minus its assets, which would make the Coke brand worth roughly $64 billion at today's close. Obviously, building and maintaining a strong brand is critical to the success and value of any organization. **Your ability to generate ongoing revenues, much like a company's, is primarily based on your personal brand and reputation.** What do you want people to associate with the "new you"? What are your core traits you want to express and again, have people remember you for?

Proficiencies: long-term asset values

A related question: On what "markets" do you want to focus your new or perhaps more appropriately "self-realized" brand? Obviously, you always want to impress those close to you, but what other constituencies might you want to meet the new you?

Proficiencies: work options; Priorities: niche visioning results

Partnering Requirements: In your context, these are whatever relationships and additional knowledge you might need to enhance your differentiation, enable change, and make your niche defensible as you chart and embark on your journey. They could include the following:

- Key relationships you want strengthened
- Classes, certifications, degrees, and so on as needed
- Professional associations, social clubs, alumni clubs, and so on that might be able to help you

Priorities: action plan outputs, niche visioning results

Management: Why are you fit to run this venture? "Because this niche is mine!" Generate a brief bio containing all relevant life experiences because they support why you will win, what makes you different, what your assets are, and what is enabling your venture. **Proficiencies: personal balance sheet**

Board of Advisors: Your board should consist of three or four people who can provide you with as objective feedback and advice as possible regarding your plan and its execution. They could easily be those folks you solicited for feedback in your personal balance sheet exercise. They can be from whatever circles of friends are circling you or whatever walk of life you are currently walking. Again, a corporate mentor or a favorite HR colleague are great potential members, depending on your current (or even past) working environment. Choosing from different groups naturally broadens the perspectives you will receive, which is **always** a good thing. Be realistic about who you think will want to join, but don't be afraid to take chances; people generally like to help others succeed. Most of all, don't select people just because you know them well. You will need as much truth as you can stand to successfully instigate long-term lasting change.

You can schedule meetings as you desire and as calendars can accommodate. Dialing in is perfectly fine, but in-person pow-wows are best. (Having your board over for drinks and dinner is a surefire way to make this happen.) Again, their purpose is to serve as sounding boards for your plan. They might add strokes of brilliance, thunderbolts that fizzle, or merely nothing at all (at least on the surface). Regardless, the power and perspective of many minds working on one is unquestionably helpful and frankly necessary. Remember, though, you, at the end of the nanosecond, are the one who makes the final decision. No matter how hard one might present his or her thoughts, you are the only chieftain present. This is an expectation that your board must be willing to deal with, and it is also your greatest responsibility. Finally, this group must respect (not necessarily agree with) each other's opinions. The last thing you want these meetings to become are egofests. **Proficiencies: feedback providers**

Financial Projections—Where It All Comes Together: If there is one document that lucidly reflects the Stockdale Paradox, this is it. No matter how long it takes, you will prevail, **but you've gotta be real first**. Numbers have a hard time lying (even those audited by certain Big Four accounting firms will inevitably pipe up). You definitely want to save for a new _____. You might even believe you will be able to put away $300 this month for _____. Then lo and behold, you find yourself rummaging through your computer bag for change to buy your "necessary" Starbucks and wondering when and how you are going to pay off the credit card-I-never-should-have-gotten you used to buy those four CDs and dinner last weekend.

Net Sum: If you are like the vast majority, you probably

- Don't know where a significant portion of your monthly money goes
- Are living near the border of financial duress
- Want help but are reticent to seek and use it because intuitively you know the process of dealing with it will be painful and will threaten your current standard of living

What is really fascinating is that the same intuitive spirit that pushes help away also recognizes the obvious fact that if you were able to understand your cash flows and could enact realistic means to, at a basic level, reallocate your funds, your stress levels would decrease dramatically. Possibly the only thing more detrimental than fear is when it is combined with laziness.

This tool has three integrated purposes:

- To gain a detailed understanding as to where your (hopefully) easily earned cash goes every month
- To establish and prioritize personal milestones you want to hit given your long-term liabilities matrix results and correlating guiding principles/action plans
- To reallocate accordingly to meet these milestones

You can generate these projections in three ways. If you are computer-friendly, you can use modules of certain applications (for example, Microsoft Money) or create your own.[1] Or you can simply sit down with a pencil and paper and write it out. Your projections, per Table 9.1, should consist of three basic sections, going from the top to the bottom of your page:

- **Income**—What you bring in through a variety of means on a monthly basis
- **Costs**—What you spend on a monthly basis
- **Savings and milestones**—What you do with your monthly leftovers, and what your plans are

TABLE 9.1 **Projections Template**

	Month 1	Month 2	Month 3	Month 4	Month 5	Month 6
Income						
Earner 1						
Earner 2						
Gifts and Other						
Property Sales						
Income Property						
Home Equity						
Portfolio						
Total Income						

TABLE 9.1　**Projections Template (continued)**

	Month 1	Month 2	Month 3	Month 4	Month 5	Month 6
Costs						
Housing						
Eating						
Commuting						
Kids						
Healthcare						
Vacations						
Clothing						
Pets						
Recreation						
Education						
Personal Business						
Big Ticket						
Debt						
Total Costs						
Starting Bank Balance						
Infusions from Savings						
Credit Card Payments						
Planned Savings						
Ending Bank Balance						
Net Change						
Starting Savings Balance						
Ending Savings Balance						
Milestones						

1　I have put together two versions (static and dynamic) of a detailed yet easy-to-follow set of spreadsheets you can download from my site to simplify this process of personal budgeting, allocation, and milestone-meeting. If you are already using your own set of spreads (kudos to you!), you might want to compare the levels of detail and my thought processes. (And if you have any suggestions to improve, please contact me!)

After you have a high-level worksheet constructed, break out each line item into its specific components; for example, "Eating" might expand to groceries, coffee/bagels/doughnuts, lunch out, and restaurants. After this has been done, start filling in your monthly columns with the appropriate information, with as much accuracy as possible. For example, if you know your power bill goes up in the winter, make sure this is reflected in the proper cost line item. You can project bonuses and other one-time income items as long as you lean on the conservative side.[2] Be sure to include credit card payments (and their annual fees) in your cost information.

When you have filled in all relevant costs, look at their total on a monthly basis. If you need to save some each month for larger payments (property taxes, tuition, vacations, and so on), spread these costs over the appropriate period so that you can add them to your monthly cost total. This total is your **personal burn rate**. In a business context, **burn rate** means the amount of cash you need to keep an organization going on a month-to-month basis. This can be an important metric because you (like many businesses) might like to have a certain number of months' burn rate in the bank as security and comfort before starting something new.

This structure has been designed to provide a level of detail that forces you to understand where you are spending your money. This said, as you fill them out, and certain payments you might know to the cent (car, rent, and so on) notwithstanding, I don't expect you to gather all receipts for the past five months and do statistical, season-adjusted regression analysis of how much you spend on "coffee/bagels/ doughnuts"; simple reflection and then gut-checked entries are all you need to provide. Be prepared for some potential surprises as to how much certain expenditures are costing you, though, particularly in relation to other arguably more important allocations of funds.

2. All income should be recorded on a post-tax basis. Like your one-time income blips, please use a believable tax rate.

The Fourth P: Plan

The most important reason this level of detail is required is to determine where and by how much you can reduce particular expenditures to free up the cash required to meet whatever investments might be required to control your niche. An amazing observation along these lines is how BIG little things can become in aggregate. Look at your monthly "coffee/bagels/doughnuts" and "lunch out" line items, for example, add them, and then multiply by 12. Where else could you use these funds? What kind of a vacation could you have? How much high-interest credit card debt could you pay off? How much could this become if you saved it for 30 years if you "retired"?[3]

Your reductions in some line items might be dramatic; they might not be. Again, what is critical to note is that by simply focusing on say, spending 10 percent less per month, on average, how much power those "saved and earned" dollars can have. How difficult is it to say to yourself as you are perusing whatever Web site or outlet you are gracing, "How can I spend ___percent less than I usually do on this kind of purchase?" It could be having a regular coffee in lieu of a latte or going to a different vendor. It could be taking the time to join a club to receive discounts on certain items. Regardless of the expenditure, and even without having to negotiate, I am sure you are already imagining ways you can easily reallocate and reduce your monthly burn.

Financing Milestones: It is this power of choice that enables the financing of your milestones and drives their acquisition. Whatever you want your targets to be—saving for the down payment on a mortgage, paying off credit card bills, saving for that once in a lifetime trip, or having six months of personal burn rate in the bank before you start transitioning to new work—these goals **must** be reflected in your spreadsheets. Hitting these magic targets

3. I must share the rule of 72 at this point. The rule goes like this: Let's say you have an investment that is paying you 6 percent per year. Dividing 6 into 72, we get 12. This is the number of years your investment will take to *double* in value with no effort by you at all. Whatever your returns are, dividing them into 72 will yield the magic number of years.

is **easily** within your grasp and ability to meet **as long as you want to make it happen.** Yes, it could take time and "sacrifice," but if the reason why you are taking these actions meets a mission, instinctively you will truly enjoy the (volitional) ride as your prioritized targets come into sight and start rapidly approaching.

Start off by focusing on three or four targets (tracking them can get a bit unruly), although if you can get into a rhythm, if your internal generator can get cranking and whirring, you can conquer many more, merely by making the requisite changes to your allocations on your spreads and then figuring out ways both to implement and maintain this new scenario. Call it creativity, call it common sense—either will do. Using your numbers to realistically set your and other stakeholder's (particularly those you love) expectations is obviously crucial and simultaneously powerful because again, numbers (unlike kids) have a hard time wiggling. Please use these targets in the last section of this plan as appropriate and in the document we will create in the next and final P.

Key Success Factors: What three or four events must happen for your new you to be presentable? Look at your top-ranked matrices outputs and guiding principles from their latest and greatest churns (post-visioning—this is utterly crucial!) and choose those that best meet this criteria. Naturally, you should also include their action plans. **Priorities: matrices, guiding principles, and action plans**

Required Investment: The first and most important step in generating this content is figuring out what kind of "funds" you will need to successfully execute your plan. As you might have surmised, the "funds" you will be requesting are much, much more than mere finances. Think of them as different kinds of support, sitting in four buckets: emotional, knowledge, spiritual, and financial. As I briefly dip into each bucket, start thinking about whose "funds" you might need access to **comfortably** meet your goals. The less you worry, the more you can scurry!

- **Emotional:** Arguably, the most important and empowering, this intangible support typically comes from family and good friends and says, "Yes, we believe in your plan, we believe you will succeed, and we will be there to support you no matter what happens. Whatever you do, you will not fail in our eyes." This kind of support might simply be the blessing of a significant other or your parents, which might be all you need.

- **Knowledge:** Per the advisory board concept, it's good to surround yourself with people whose experience and knowledge of life and potential work options can be immensely helpful, particularly if your plan is taking you in a different direction; the compounding power of your network is indisputably one of your greatest assets. You want these investors solely for their knowledge, not merely because they can open doors for you. The latter might come, but only after you have gained their trust and confidence (that only a presentation can elicit).

- **Spiritual:** Whatever additional dosing you might need from a higher power (or powers), seek it. Be it a standard weekend visit, daily prayer, becoming one with nature, or endlessly looping your favorite CD, if you want to include this incredibly powerful kind of support, solicit it!

- **Financial:** Raising money should be the least important objective of this exercise. If people whose support you need coincidentally have a couple extra dollars in the bank, that's great. Should such support follow to enable or accelerate your goals, that's even better. This said, PLEASE don't complete this step with the idea or intent that the foolproof, money-back guaranteed presentation format presented in the last P should be used to this end.

There is a saying, "It takes a village to raise a child." I'd like to build on this on with the observation, "It takes a network to sustain them." What you are basically looking to create or reinforce is a network of support (as opposed to a "support network") that you can access **if needed** as you execute your plan. Make a list of at most five people or couples whose support you'd like, and delineate the kind of investment you seek, again trying to avoid the jingly one. Your advisory board can be a good place to look for investors, and fortunately, there shouldn't be conflicts of interest in this context.

The Exit Strategy/Key Milestones

Take this heading literally. Your exit strategy should reflect the when and how you will leave whatever facet(s) of life are holding you back from working your passion. More specifically, what key milestones must you run over to make this process work? These milestones could be related to your partnering activities—finishing up a course you need to get into a new line of work, or researching the hell out of the _____ industry—or something tactical like having at minimum two (passion-pressing) offers from other firms or putting feelers out in other parts of your current employer. They could be financial, per the burn rate example earlier. They could be geographic—researching and finding the house you've always dreamed of in Portland, Oregon and then building work around that geography. Whatever your milestones, make sure they are practical, realistic, and any associated costs are reflected in your pro-forma. **Priorities: guiding principles, niche visioning results; Plan: partnering requirements, financing milestones**

THE RULE OF THE SIX PS

Don't worry. This is not the sister (or even distant relative) of the Five Ps already hitting you up for more aggravation. The rule of the Six Ps was conceived somewhere in the military and reads like this: "Prior Proper Planning Prevents Piss-Poor Performance." Somewhere along your LifeTime, you might have also encountered the converse: "Prior Proper Planning **Promotes** Piss-Poor Performance." Regardless of interpretation, the key is making sure your plan is "proper," and proper means **thorough**. Your plan should be iterated a couple of times. It should be reflected on, set aside and allowed to simmer for a while, and then revisited with fresh thoughts that inevitably put you closer to finishing before you have even begun. It is amazing to see how much of a plan can come together by merely sitting down and starting to work on it. You might have no idea how to develop potentially critical parts, although the mere act of starting the process—taking that first step down an unknown corridor—can be cathartic, liberating, and actually FUN!

The funny thing about planning is that by merely committing your focus to the process of developing a plan, you are already 80 percent toward realizing whatever goal you are trying to meet as long as you can imagine how the different parts of that process come together. It doesn't matter if you are hiking in unknown terrain, driving from Baton Rouge, Louisiana to Billings, Montana, or transitioning from job X to your life's work. The fear, anxiety, stress, and worry of the trip falls to the floor if you have a plan, particularly one that is self-generated. Plans, this one in particular, are a magnified version of a concept introduced in the prior P; it is tremendously easier to get what you want if you know what you want. And by this time, you might have a pretty good idea of both knowing what you want and knowing how to get it. All you have to do now is start writing, and per Valerie's example that follows, it really isn't all that difficult!

VALERIE: CASE STUDY

Plan

The following is a slightly edited version of Valerie's life summary.

Mission: To give of herself selflessly and always be there when needed. To bring sunshine to people's lives and her local community.

What Is Enabling My Venture:

- Better quality of life/less pressure: Flexible commute, decent work hours with no weekends, salary (versus commissions), working with smart people and for a solid company.
- Identifying my strengths and passions toward a locally based business model.
- Perceived need for a child-facility in my city.

What I Will Do: Working for a larger, stable, yet dynamic publicly held company.

Wealth: Financial stability = house, car, savings, and slush fund for travel and treats.

Success: Inner happiness and peace of mind, and less stress from work and other commitments. Love/partnership... close and healthy relationships with family and intimate friends. Stay-at-home mother involved in many community activities.

How I Will Make Money: High base salary/guaranteed bonus. Stock purchase plan and three weeks + vacation. Flexible working location to offset potential commuting.

Why I Will Win/What Makes Me Different: My work experiences, network, people skills, professionalism, attention to detail, and organizational abilities put me at a tremendous advantage and provide strong differentiation versus anyone else who shares my mission and potential releases. My long-term liabilities—wanting children, a secure financial state, and time to travel—add to this state of uniqueness.

How I Will Market Myself: My personal brand is based on persistence, sincerity, integrity, and genuineness. I want to focus my brand on markets that will help me meet my earlier milestones—movers and shakers/power centers in local community. These include the local political scene, business owners, Chamber of Commerce members, and boards of local nonprofits.

Partnering Requirements: Chamber of Commerce involvement, classes (QuickBooks).

Management: 15 years of sales success balanced by numerous leading positions in a variety of local volunteering efforts including organizing auctions, a Fourth of July parade, and sitting on non-profit boards.

Advisory Board: Mom/Dad, Matt, Don, Mayor Snell, Rhonda.

Financial Milestones: Great savings. None needed at present.

Key Success Factors: Having a child. Doing well at my next job. Being able to jump on the right opportunities that come my way.

Required Investment: To initially carry this off, I will need support from the following:

Mom/Dad	Emotional and knowledge
Matt	Knowledge
Don	Knowledge and emotional

Exit Strategy:
- Leave my current employer at the end of the month; negotiate package.
- Contact my network of software friends within the next five business days.

continues

- Talk to headhunters within the next five business days.
- Search for "fit" organizations within 30 to 40 miles within the next two weeks.
- Pursue as many interviews as possible.
- When settled, research local options.

This is a nicely crafted "executing your life" type of summary. It's concise, precise, and to the point. I can't adequately stress the importance of being succinct! This was the first time I had read Valerie's mission, and I believe she is right on target. She can deliver sunshine like few others can, her skill sets complement it, her long-term categories (both assets and liabilities) are geared for it, her meta-passions breathe it, and her releases reflect it. The only thing she needs to do now is figure out how to make her numbers work. What is particularly amazing about this mission statement is how quickly she was able to generate it—no more than two hours total focused on the process—although these hours were interspersed by a few days to just think and iterate on the questions that the process asked. Although your mission typically envelops you like skin, repeated exfoliations over the course of days, weeks, or even months might be required to bring your essence to the surface.

Valerie's enabling trends are also spot on. She realizes her life situation has changed, and **thus her work needs to evolve, too;** these acknowledgements are obviously critical to making change happen. I also like them because they are pragmatic. Valerie realizes that given her current financial needs, per her priorities and pro-forma, she is most comfortable joining the corporate ranks again, which she is adept at doing. This said, her passions and mission point directly at doing something local and possibly charitable, and her inclusion of a possible need for a business she would thrive at as an enabling trend is perfect.

Her "What I Will Do" section reflects this short- to medium-term focus on generating corporate wealth, as she defines it, although if she can focus her passions and mission to meet her definition of success, again I'd bet this what I will do section will change. Her "How I Will Make Money" and "How I Will Win" sections are plugged in from prior deliverables, although I'd like to see more from her long-term experience assets here. Her brand identity is also taken from her personal balance sheet, and I like her selection of markets she is targeting with her brand to meet her mission and definition of success. On this note, the absence of any corporate reference in this context might unconsciously answer a question posed in the prior P as to where she thinks she will find her match. Her partnering requirements are nicely tactical and pertinent, and depending on what should happen down the road, she might need to become involved in additional organizations and enroll in more courses.

Valerie's management bio is also well-tuned to the needs of her summary because it mentions her professional successes, but more importantly, it appropriately presents her relevant releases. Her pro-forma (which you can download if you'd like to have a look) is well-thought out, honest, and includes a special savings entry to start putting away money to make her mission goals possible. Her required investment and board of advisors are manageable and realistic, and she was easily able to solicit their involvement. Finally, and most importantly, her exit strategy reflects the culmination of all prior entries. She had already explored different positions within her current firm but for various reasons decided it was not the place she wanted to be. She wisely realized it was much better for her to potentially be without income (depending on what kind of package she could negotiate) and upbeat until she found another job rather than continuing to be miserable and trying to look for work on the side. Again, Valerie was proactive, tactical, and decisive with paramount focus on her short-term needs, but with her mission still in mind.

Great job, Valerie!

CHAPTER 10

THE FIFTH P: PROVE

HOW DO YOU FUND YOUR PLAN?

The proof that any plan, yours being no exception, has what it takes to succeed can quickly be determined by its ability to get funded. If people believe in what you are building enough to give you their money, the plan's chances for success must be better than good. Probably the most enjoyable, satisfying, and perhaps surprising part of the entire process is when you present your plan to your investors for their support. This is when you will **and must** unabashedly show off your understanding and alignment of who you are, what your mission is, how you will win in a different way, and what the enabling numbers are that will strategically and tactically lead you to your goals. The pleasure of merely liberating the energy, focus, and commitment you have applied getting to this point in the process is almost unbeatable. Most importantly, your belief in your plan, its underpinnings, and your abilities to realize your niche will be magnetic. **People like dealing with confident and impassioned people.**

Some Stockdale Paradox expectations are in order now, too. From experience, aspects of this P (Prove) can put you on the defensive, can be angst-ridden, and curiously, can be lonely. Let me briefly explain these dynamics. There will forever be holes in any plan and potential disagreement on key points. Disagreement is not a bad thing. At worst, you may need to re-examine your assumptions and perhaps come out with a new rendering, which tactfully side-steps or no-holds barred broaches setbacks of prior versions. At minimum, disagreement gives you one additional shield (or lance) of preparedness for your next appearance. You should expect dis-agreement, but remember that you are THE expert in this partic-ular arena: Nobody knows the entirety of your niche better. You have done your research, assembled your advisory board members for their knowledge and experience, and know your numbers colder than a New England breeze in January.

It is also fair to observe that after you and the others have agreed on a time and place, simply waiting for the presentations to happen can be a bit anxiety-ridden. This is normal. You don't know what is going to happen, you really want this funding, and you know you will need to sell your plan. You fret and worry and are mentally besieged by additions that your presentation must include to make your pitch stick. You can also easily imagine spilling coffee on your investor, tripping on the carpet, or a thousand other potential X-Factors that will most certainly cast you and your plan in a bad light. To jump shift a little, don't worry about the details. As long as you can present your plan's skeleton, main muscles, and brains clearly and concisely, any wrinkles, pimples, scars, or acts of gravity will quickly fade away.

A final emotion you may experience is one of isolation because you are leading your foray into truly uncharted territory. This is a really fascinating dilemma. On one hand, you are giddy because you know where your life is going—work, geographies, finances, and so on—and you can almost feel the satisfying jolt of whacking your passion ball over the Green Monster in the Boston Red Sox ball park. On the other hand, you are the only person on this planet who understands your niche with the particular depth of knowledge, experience, and planning, which oddly can make you feel remote or separated from the world around you. Don't worry about this either, because this feeling is completely normal;. This "island in the stream" sensation will dissipate as your mind and body start moving through the execution process, beginning with your presentations.

Incidentally, you might also be encountering another emotion, which could have quietly started to snowball midway through the last P: a feeling of overpowering urgency to start implementing your plan NOW—everything and everyone else should follow or get out of your way. You have tallied your founder's stock, and in the process of filling in your spreadsheets, you have realized both the mammoth power and purpose of time—your LifeTime more specifically—and you want to start making changes today. Please do, by the way, because soliciting support is best done simultaneously, not sequentially, in conjunction with executing your plan. Just be open to your investors' concerns and willing to integrate their requests. The point here is that you don't want to become too evangelical or rabid with your potential funders, because the last thing you want to do is alienate them **before** you make your request. It's not that your presentation won't knock their socks off. As we used to say in college, the easiest (and quickest) way to remove other people's clothing is to have them do it for you.

PROFESSIONAL FUNDRAISING 101

A brief primer on fundraising is in order. My varied and sundry experiences of raising money in a variety of contexts has given me a few insights you may be able to use in the process of securing support for your plan:

- **Investors should invest in management, not merely an idea**—Ideas come and go just like your 15 minutes of fame. Investors, if they are smart, should know who is managing the ship before putting their resources behind the next expedition to locate Atlantis. Credibility is absolutely critical to these ends. Again, credibility is the asset that new businesses use to secure their funding. Because this is your plan, of your making, no one is better qualified in the world to manage it and your funders' support.

- **The ability to execute trumps who get to market first**—In this case, you are already first to your market because no one can possibly be going after your niche armed with the differentiation bestowed by your specific assets, liabilities, priorities, and mission. Yes, other people might already be selling decorative wall covers over the Internet, and if so, they have done two favors for you already: established a market for your offering, and provided a bar that your passion can easily clear. The essential question is this: Can you execute on your plan? The answer should be obvious.

- **Investors like to see the fruits of their funding**— Because the support you are looking to galvanize is not financial, figure out how you can let your investors follow and track how their investment is faring. It could be a simple e-mail update on a monthly basis, or it could be a grand announcement or a bottle of (budgeted) bubbly when you hit certain milestones. Regardless of the medium, you must keep those who are giving you their support in the loop. You might be surprised about the impact that a quarterly return statement or some other update can have on future investment requirements.

- **Thank them**—Consider investors' allotments of their LifeTime to help you as the greatest gift you can request and receive. **Do not squander or take any of these relationships for granted!** Thank whoever helps you, particularly those who might have made introductions to potential advisory board members. In this context, the act of thanking someone is a conveyance of respect for their time and effort. And don't forget the power of receiving a hand-written thank-you note in this day of autoresponse e-mail and laser-printed signatures. Such a simple and personal device, used for centuries, is quickly becoming virtually obsolete. Thank them from your heart, because you are asking for some of theirs.

"ALL I WANT ARE THE FACTS, MA'AM"

With these observations in mind, you will use a presentation format, successfully employed in the venture capital (VC) game, whose structure can be relevant to presenting yourself and your plan for personal funding. VC presentations can run the gamut from lackadaisical to laconic, depending on the nature of the venture capitalists, their interest, and your relationship with them. Most sessions are quite civil, although the occasional screaming matches do happen. Like all investors, VCs like to gather particular data quickly, efficiently, and sometimes with little regard to your planned agenda. Consequently, understanding the kind of information they need to make their decisions and then concisely presenting this information is vital to making this process smooth and most importantly, under your control.

Odds are, you are probably thinking, "Why on earth would I ever want to present to a money-grubbing venture capitalist?" The answer (unless you are a budding entrepreneur and you'd like the practice) is twofold. First, it is the **process** of creating the presentation and the thought behind its **content** and **sequence** that are important to understand in this context. Second, you are looking to raise funds, and doing this implicitly means that you must **ask** for them. Using this format makes the actual process of "the asking" an easy one and reduces the odds that your request will be passed on. Raising these critical funds needs to be as risk-free a proposition as possible.

Another good question might also be percolating: Why do I necessarily **need** to present anything? Why can't I simply send my investors my life summary and walk them through it? You shouldn't do that for three reasons. First, many investors don't have the time or focus to read anything longer than those teaser info-clips located on the front page of the *Wall Street Journal*. Their ability to understand and remember anything noteworthy about your plan (versus the 20 other documents grumbling in their In box) is meager at best. This may not be the case depending on the kind of investors and your relationships with them, although occasionally you might need to move yourself up their prioritization ladder to really get the support you are asking for.

Second, people learn in different ways, and the ability to both visually view concepts and simultaneously listen to their description is a very efficient means of educating your audience. This need to educate is a critical ingredient to digest because its flavor should infuse all layers of your verbal and written content. You, the expert in your niche, intrinsically need to **educate** (versus sell) your investors on the particulars of your plan, regardless of how intelligent or accomplished they are. It is only by properly educating a potential partner that he or she will feel comfortable doing the deal.

The Fifth P: Prove

The last reason is simply to be able to leave your investor with something tangible and memorable from your interaction. Always bring at least one printed version with you to leave behind; the odds that your investor will print an e-mailed copy *post-facto* are notably small. Simply put, the visual reminder of simply seeing your documents patiently sitting on his or her desk can be what makes or breaks your investor to call up his or her friends at that chocolate shop you've always wanted to manage to see if they might need any help. Getting a physical place on your investors' desks—even just temporarily—and politely forcing them to clear you off is a useful way to get on their "list of things to do today."

The following format and sequence have been designed to answer questions your investors might have with your plan with ample opportunity to drill down as they see fit. Who controls this "degree of detail" is a critical distinction. More than a couple aspiring entrepreneurs have been denied by immediately going from the 30,000-foot view to The Land of the Troglodytes in 3 seconds or less. If the sudden drop didn't kill interest, the impact surely did. If your investors have questions, they will ask them. Don't try to fill in dead space or pauses with any more information than what is needed. Remember, this is **their** time they are giving you to spend to a floating point. If that point is hit, the investors will (and justifiably should) take the reins, which instinctively is not preferable. You want to control the cadence and content of the presentation, at least until you've delivered the last page.

You can create your presentation in two ways, depending on your degree of computer proficiency. If you are digitally inclined, you may have used an application called Microsoft PowerPoint; even if you have used it only once, you are all set.[1] If not, simply find some 8 x by 11 pieces of paper, turn them on their side, and sharpen your ever-present pencil. We will be making less than

1. For your convenience, you can download a preformatted version from my Web site.

10 pages, or slides as they are called, for this presentation, also known as a deck, with minimal need for artistry. Don't worry if your handwriting or graphic creation capabilities are like mine.

Slides are extremely effective because they present content in bites that are easy to swallow. They typically have a title, which takes up roughly the top fifth of the page, centered or left-side justified, in larger letters. The title summarizes the data on that slide. The boldfaced text following the number of each slide below is the suggested title of that slide; "Mission" would be the title of the first slide. You can also include a title page if you'd like, embellished or simplified to your liking. You have already created all the data you need for this exercise. At this stage of the process, **how** your content is packaged becomes tantamount to your success. Again, I have tried my best to defrock the deck of extraneous business jargon.

Are you ready? Here we go!

SLIDE #1: MISSION

The first slide of content usually contains a mission statement. Not to state the obvious, but you should do the same. Include only your mission statement and nothing more. You may want to include a copy of your passion graphic as an appendix item so that you can quickly refer to it if the investors have questions about how you came to know your mission.

SLIDE #2: WHAT IS ENABLING MY VENTURE?

The next slide typically focuses on high-level trends that are coalescing to create the demand for this opportunity. What is important to convey is how these combined forces create an unquestionable need for your niche. To this end, graphically displaying your trends coming together and creating your niche visitioning outputs (your venture) can be extremely powerful. You can illustrate them any way you'd like, but an example of a simple format is shown in Figure 10.1. Simply copying the text from your plan into the placeholders might be all you need to do here.

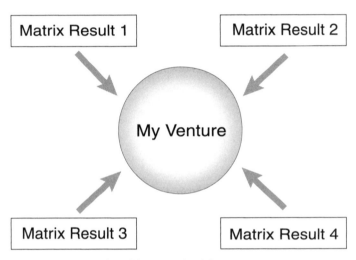

FIGURE 10.1   Diagram of enabling trends slide.

SLIDE #3: MY NICHE

This is where the product or service panacea that will quash any unmet customer needs is presented, typically in terms of its features and benefits. This is one of the most important slides of the deck because it's where you will lay out what you are going to do (or might have even started doing), in prioritized, tactical fashion to realize your niche visioning outputs. Cull into this slide what you will do, how you will make money, and what your most prominent guiding principles and action plans are.

SLIDE #4: WHY WILL I WIN?

What assets do you solely possess that will enable you to capitalize on your converging trends? In a business context, this could
consist of intellectual property such as patents, key management,
research, or relationships with critical partners or customers. In
your case, it is merely your personal balance sheet, in all its stunning glory. Again, you want to convey how no one else can go
after and secure your niche. This slide, in combination with the
next one, is designed to instill confidence in your investors that
their funding will help you realize your milestones and simultaneously minimize risks of failure.

SLIDE #5: MANAGEMENT

This slide is fairly self-explanatory. Management provides a
quick-yet-not-so-dirty synopsis of their work experiences and
conquests to date. In your version, try to focus on your patterns
of releases and meta-passions and how they tie to your mission.
These patterns will highlight your relevant successes.

SLIDE #6: WHAT IS MY TIMETABLE?

This slide typically lays out projected time and costs required
to develop a new product, market it, and generate enough sales so
that the company requires no further investment for operating
purposes. This information is typically presented as milestones
with the accumulated investment needed to smack them. You
want to present similar data: milestones and any associated costs
if appropriate. Look at your financing milestones, and present them
chronologically with sums as needed. Also, I strongly suggest bait-
ing the final hook by casually mentioning these milestones came
about in the process of generating your financial projections
(which you have included as an appendix item). If your investors

aren't impressed enough by the presentation, seeing your niche come together with the stolid rationality of numbers may require the presence of a resuscitator.

SLIDE #7: KEY SUCCESS FACTORS

This page's content can also come directly from your life summary. Again, what are the three or four critical matrices or niche visioning outputs, and their respective guiding principles and action plans, that need to happen? Finding new work in new city _____ with a salary level of $55,000 by October 1. Finishing up your home inspector's license process by June 1 of next year. Paying down your credit card debt by $300 per month until you are debt free, or putting $300 per month in a special account to fulfill your long-term liability of an Italian vacation.

SLIDE #8: BOARD OF ADVISORS

This slide is important because it reinforces your understanding of the different factors you might need to deal with and the resources to draw on to execute your plan. Fundamentally, it shows how your network of support reduces risks of all shapes and sizes, and even though you may never actually need to reach out to any of them, merely having the capability to solicit their advice and support provides an additional layer of comfort to any investor. You might want to delineate your relationship with each board member and the kind of knowledge you desire.

SLIDE #9: REQUIRED INVESTMENT AND USE OF FUNDS

In dollarland, this slide lays out how much money you think you will need to reach certain milestones. In your case, per the required investment section of your life summary, money alone should probably be the last thing you hope to (directly) receive from your investors. Include your list of investors and what kind of support (emotional, knowledge, or spiritual) you need to meet your objectives.

This is the slide when you "make the ask." It's when you lift your veil, open your kimono, and request whatever support, or perhaps more appropriately, **access** to whatever funds you require to meet your milestones. (Note: This could be a novel, although not entirely romantic, way to propose to someone.) Your request probably should be something practical yet not overtly detailed.

"Honey, all I am asking from you is your emotional support and patience while I make this transition. It could be difficult for us financially, yet I know, deep down in my gut, this is the right move for me."

"Mr. Montrose, all I am requesting is having the ability to access your knowledge of the _____ industry as I make my transition."

"Dad, you have always been there for me—emotionally, financially, and with your knowledge. All I ask from you now is your blessing and knowledge as I make this transition. I know we may disagree on certain points, but in my gut, I know this is the right thing for me to be doing."

This is also the point where you should discretely open up the discussion to questions and feedback. Be prepared to answer or provide detail to whatever unknowns or uncertainties may still linger. You might field some particularly tough questions from those closest to you, and your request may not be granted the first or even second time around. Those you love and who love you can often be the most difficult sell of all. You might be asked to go back and do more research, answer more questions, or polish certain parts of your plan. Comments might lead to new understandings that may change parts of your plan and funding requirements. Know though, inevitably and iteratively, you will win.

KEEPING IT IN THE FAMILY

A relevant question often emerges at this juncture: I know my family loves me and will support me in whatever I do. Why do I need to go through this whole presentation song and dance? A couple of reasons deserve some attention.

First, there's the notion of pride. There's pride in seeing your kids, spouse, or significant other striving to be the best they can be and proactively broaching this tricky and potentially frightening process with a rational, researched, and financially sound plan behind them. There's also the pride of realizing no matter how many mistakes the **mutual** "you" may have made, you are still coming back to them for their blessing and guidance, even though they know full well you'd be able to get by without it.

The second reason is that you may actually need their support like never before. Even with a firm belief in your core, having the power of parents and others behind you can make execution significantly easier. **It is a mature individual who realizes that he or she alone can do great things; approaching a mission as a team, though, can create extraordinary achievements.**

> "So what now?
> Do we shake hands and go our separate ways?
> Or do I open my mind and follow you into the haze?"
>
> —Minor Threat

You have completed the process of the Five Ps. No matter where you are (particularly if you are on a plane and the captain has just asked everyone to fasten their seatbelts), I implore you to rise on your haunches, take a deep bow, and treat yourself to something delectable, caffeinating, intoxicating, or all three. You deserve it! You are already **80%** of the way toward living your dreams—and living in the time of your life—as you downshift two gears for power, destroy the accelerator, and start to implement your plan.

From here on out, you should allocate the vast majority of your energy and focus toward executing your plan, bearing three critical points in mind:

- You will inevitably be the recipient of both amazingly good and bad X-Factors, probably just when you least expect them. Be prepared to integrate their influence into your plan and (this is essential) be open to whatever new directions they may take you.

- Your priorities can and will change: incrementally as years pass, in nine-month increments, or in a heartbeat or two. To accommodate these shifting priorities, you might want **and need** to change how you release your passions into your working life.

- Life, on your terms, is your oyster! Suck it dry, and be ready for those pearls!

The purpose of the Five Ps is to give you an understanding of your mission and passions, assets and liabilities, and key priorities so that you can start making incremental, iterative, and illuminated changes to your journey. It can be difficult, painful, and arduous to undo the intricate and delicate webs you have been spinning for most of your life to make room for your new cocoon. This reconstruction will at minimum require acknowledgement and quite probably initiative, which is the topic of the next and decisive chapter.

VALERIE: CASE STUDY

The Fifth P: Prove

Valerie's presentations went nicely and, although drilled on some aspects, everyone was impressed and predictably gave her their support. I believe she is well on her way to living on her terms, and her game has now become one of methodical execution. To be clear, she is not optimized yet and probably won't be for a while, certain X-Factors notwithstanding. Having a glimpse of her next destination and a discrete plan to get her there, however, has re-energized her beyond her wildest expectations. She commented, "I know where I am going, and I am happy with where I am going because it meets my mission."

(As a postscript, Valerie was able to find and start a job at a top-notch software/services employer within two months of leaving her old digs, from whom she was able to secure a month of severance. She likes her new boss, can work from home two days per week, has 9 to 5 hours, only needs to commute 30 minutes each way, expects to work no weekends, and will need to travel to New York City, which she loves to do, on the corporate quarter, four times per year. The only downside is that half of her projected compensation is commission-based, which might impact her hours and desire to become less stressed.)

CHAPTER 11

HOW DO I PREPARE MYSELF
FOR THIS CHANGE?

ANY JOURNEY

Any journey—from a quick trip to the store, a weeklong hike in the mountains, to making a life transition of any scale—can be tough. There will inevitably be hang-ups, things won't go as planned, and your path can be waylaid easily at many points along the way. An unexpected detour on Main Street due to road construction, days of straight rain making backpacks too heavy to carry, or the realization that you really want to leave _____, Inc., LLC, or LLP, move to the other side of the world, and use your unique set of talents and experiences to exploit your niche. X-Factors abound and **creativity** to deal with these unforeseen events is required to meet your objectives. Looking back from your destination, this intrinsic capability that has defined our species was significantly to thank for the success of your voyage.

"Creativity?" you say. "I haven't got a creative bone in my body. Maybe that's why I'm stuck." Believe it or not, you are incredibly creative in your own way. You might create through music, software development, cooking, or by figuring out new ways to make processes work more efficiently. Some poor souls even like to get creative with accounting rules. (Stay away from them!) Intuitively, whatever you are passionate about, whatever you can't get enough of, whatever you choose to explore and understand the essence of—therein lies the source of your creative juices.

Look around you for a moment. Does anything require electricity to run? The simple act of flipping a switch and turning on a light took years, even decades, to come about. Do you think Edison had to be creative to make this happen? Incredibly so. Was luck involved? More than likely, to some degree, despite hundreds of attempts. Looking back, though, what was it that expanded Edison's creativity and generated the scenarios that enabled an extraordinary event to occur? That's simple. It was his mission to light the world and his passion for invention.

Let's look at another example: the invention of the mass-produced car. Any idea how many times Henry Ford went bankrupt trying to iterate on his concept of a production line that sucked in raw metal at one end and spat out affordable cars on the other? Twice. He bet his farm two times, and two times he lost it. Imagine putting everything you own behind an idea—your investments, your 401(k) or IRA, your home, and most precious of all, your LifeTime—and watching them go away... **twice**. Imagine the inner turmoil, the doubt, the social stigma, and the heated family conversations Henry surely endured. What pushed him through? It was his mission to make cars everyone could buy and his passion for process. In the end, of course, Henry prevailed and triumphed to a scale most of us can only imagine. What a journey he had!

More dramatic souls might cast these journeys as ordeals, with a recognizable pattern of peaks and valleys as the story unfolds. A favorite read in high school, *The Hero with a Thousand Faces* by Joseph Campbell, does an excellent job identifying these themes, which, as the title hints, have been repeated in literature throughout time and across cultures. Heroes are not your typical muscle-popping, leather-clad, and fearless protagonists who speak with random foreign accents. Rather, the hero figure is all too mortal. Heroes are emotional, often weak in body, and are besieged by internal demons and doubts. In many cases, they must flee their house or country with nothing but the clothes on their backs, forced into undertaking their missions by circumstances beyond their control. They are blatantly unprepared, and their odds of success seem dismally small.

As their journey unfolds, our heroes are confronted by a host of nasty and deadly obstacles—furious storms, wild animals, monsters, armies, and the wrath of collection agencies as they are understandably distracted from paying their credit card bills on time. Somehow, by providence, luck, a good dose of ingenuity, but most of all, **a belief in themselves and their mission**, they survive. They slay the dragon, free the prince, and beat the credit agencies into submission. Does this plot sound familiar? *Lord of the Rings*-esque perchance? A rip-off of *The Iliad*? My story? *Candide*? The alcoholic named Jim and his son? *The Divine Comedy*? Sharon Stone? Even *Caddyshack*, by far the most influential piece of media on my upbringing, plays by these (winter) rules.

What is striking about this plotline is the growth and learning that the heroes undergo as they battle their way through the myriad forces set against them. They emerge from their volitional pursuit transformed and rejuvenated, with a renewed sense of life, priority, purpose, and happiness. The film *Hidalgo*, the story of Francis Hopkins' epic horse race across the Arabian Desert, provides another great case in point. Hopkins, played by Viggo Morgenson, enters the race as America's best long-distance rider, although he has been haunted by a weakness for the bottle dealing with his mixed Native American/Caucasian heritage. It is only by committing himself to facing the overwhelming small odds of success and pushing himself and his trusty mustang to their physical and spiritual limits that he befriends his past, loses his flask, wins the race, and returns a calm and contented cowboy. With his Indian family trinket proudly dangling from his vest, he uses his winnings to buy back the freedom—in fact, the very existence— of the Spanish mustang on American soil, as they were to be slaughtered. In fact, according to the "What happened to Hopkins" text in the movie's closing moments, Hopkins became a staunch advocate for the Spanish mustang until his death in 1951.

Although certain elements of this story have undoubtedly been fabricated by Hollywood, the central theme is obvious: "That which does not kill us makes us stronger," or perhaps an even better Nietzsche-ism, **"He who has a why to live for can endure almost any how."** The first time I read this quote—on the book flap of the memoirs of an Auschwitz survivor—really underscored its fundamental power.

The reason these few words command prolific attention is their simplicity and intrinsic truth. You get it the first time you read it, and implicitly, you agree. Stripping away the social veneer of our Starbucks' addictions, shopping mall infatuations, and other "things I can't do without," you know deep down that if things suddenly took a dramatic turn for the worse, you would survive. This is a critical takeaway whose importance will become increasingly apparent over the next few sections. Simply put, if you can define your mission, your power to meet it will become potentially unstoppable.

THE JOURNEY OF LIFE

"Life is all about the journey," a popular saying goes. Or, per a Delta Airlines ad campaign, "After all, life is a journey." In fact, I'd argue that life is **THE** journey. Yes, you may be fortuned to have the LifeTime to hit whatever goals you set, but there will **always** be more goals to meet. This is a plain fact about the human condition—you will always keep striving for something, and in the process, will constantly be embarking on new journeys of various durations and difficulties. Quick question: What version of your personal operating system are you using now? It could be an upgrade resultant of new job, new city, new degree, new significant other, new pet, new insight… however you want to define it. Are you happy with where your current journeys are taking you? How have prior ones ended? Your climaxes have probably ranged from awe-inspiring enlightenments as to the meaning of (your?) life to hair-pulling and frustrating thoughts of "Never again will I…."

This, of course, is how life works. Life is an iterative process, and the remarkable thing is that no matter how many times you may have been slammed in the face, here you are again, giving it another shot. It is your **indomitable** ability to tap your core and start a new journey **regardless** of age, condition, level of indebtedness, and so on that you simply cannot forget. You might choose not to, depending on a variety of factors; the important thing is that you **can**.

Navigating the Five Ps may very well resemble an ordeal, with a structure much like that described previously. You'll have obstacles that you and others erect. You'll experience peaks of confidence and understanding and canyons of question and doubt. You'll be privy to unexpected bumps in the road, some requiring a jacked-up 4x4 and others you can endure in a Mini Cooper. And I can say with the utmost certainty that there will be tremendous learning and growth, perhaps more than you are ready to handle. Like Homer, myself, and Danny Noonan, all completely unfit on the surface for our respective gauntlets, you might be tested and retested, and then tested again to see if your belief in your mission and core has what it takes to win. "I wish it need not have happened in my time," said Frodo, as he started to imagine how dramatically his life would change because of his possession of the master ring. "So do I," replied Gandalf, the wizard. "And so do all who live to see such times. But that is not for them to decide. **All we have to decide is what to do with the time that is given us.**"

WHY?

A good question inevitably comes up, "Why does this self-imposed duress **need** to happen? Why can't I just keep living and learning the way I currently am?" A useful means to explain why you should focus on life stuff **now** predictably comes from three questions raised when looking at potential investment strategies:

- What kind of returns (that is, growth, income, and so on) do you want to realize from your investments?
- When do you want to start seeing those dividend checks hitting your account?
- And, above all, what sort of risk tolerance do you have to particular kinds of investments?

In your personal model, you decide the nature of your returns—growth, learning, life and work happiness, better relationships with your family, more money from reloading with passion, whatever. And let's assume you would like to see your life account grow quickly, end-of-year tax planning momentarily kicked to the side. The real question is one of **risk**, broken down into two classes. First is **market risk**—how much volatility exists in the overall market? Second is **investment risk**—how comfortable are you investing in this particular opportunity versus the bevy of other available options? Market risk can be compared to your openness to step outside your comfort zone and confront whatever monstrosities surely lay in wait as you iterate toward your Holy Grail. Investment risk is simply how much LifeTime you want to dedicate to this endeavor, versus the multitude of other potential allocations. With any luck, you've minimized market risk concerns by the observation that you are **not** a cat, as defined earlier. Your focus should now center on the investment risk aspect of this potential objection.

Let's say you have $100 to invest, and for the sake of example, let's pick a simple investment option: a savings account. Would you want to invest it all now to start accruing interest immediately, or would you rather put in $10 per year for the next 10 years? As a more topical example, let's expand your options to an IRA or 401(k) and ask the same question—would you like to invest more now to realize returns that can be exponentially larger than if you strung out your infusions? An analogy should be becoming apparent. Presuming you are in this game for the long haul, the more you can invest NOW, the better off you will be in the future. The same applies to how you choose to invest your LifeTime. Or as a Native American saying goes, "The more care you give your path in its beginning, the nicer it will be as you age." The risks of making this investment might seem large, particularly because you will need to prioritize the Five Ps and their outputs into your already frenetic schedule. These opportunity costs pale, though, when compared to the certain suboptimal returns that doing nothing will most certainly generate. Nothing ventured, nothing gained. You can hedge investments, but you can't hedge life!

YOUR COMPETITIVE ADVANTAGE

Unlike the anonymous Hobbit-Turned-Savior of Middle Earth, you have access to the knowledge and power of others' experience as they started recharting their paths. Borrowing from the Boy Scout tag line, the key to the success of your expedition is "being prepared." Or, for the testosterone crowd, "The battle is won or lost before it starts," as Sun Tzu mused. Emotionally, financially, and commitment-wise, you must be ready for the potential gradations of change you will be instigating on yourself and quite possibly others. Any potential impacts the Five Ps might be able to unleash will be significantly dampened if you aren't ready or aware of what is to come.

The following sections deal with three common issues you should address in preparing for your journey. They might be complete nonsense or simply not apply to you. A few might hit so close to home that you might think your firewall has failed, your 128-bit encrypted passwords have cracked, Spyware catchers have been defeated, and your online diary and bank accounts have been hacked. Please give these concepts as much attention, focus, and action as they need. In fact, you may want to put the book down at each section's close, reflect on its message for a spell, and then take the appropriate next guided and principled steps. You **must** feel comfortable and prepared for what is to come. Ask yourself, "Am I ready to continue?" If your gut says, "Yes," plunge ahead. If not, whatever utility the Five Ps might provide will be compromised, perhaps substantially, because sooner or later even just one of these topics can really mess things up.

Canyonlands

I have had the amazing fortune to have hiked into some of America's most beautiful canyons: The Grand One, Bryce and Zion, some random canyon where I almost died, and my personal

How Do I Prepare Myself for This Change?

favorite, Havasu Canyon, also located in Arizona. My experiences have revealed that being in a canyon is not necessarily a bad thing. Canyons can be extraordinarily stunning as the light, colors, and shadows move and meld. They can be terrifyingly dangerous should a flash flood suddenly appear. Most memorably, they are a remarkable place to ponder and reflect. Being enveloped by these enormous waves of smooth and layered rock provides a removed, inescapable, and safe space to ruminate and work things through. The feelings is sort of like those insights your brain provides when you lose yourself in a good run, but on a much larger scale.

You should explore three discernable canyons as you make the change from working a job to working your life. The first maps out your past and future expectations to ensure that when your snowball starts rolling, not even the heat generated as it approaches the speed of sound will cause it to melt. The second is lovingly called the standard of living trap, a shady crevice from which many a credit report has not come out alive. The last is that fearful ravine named *commitment*, through which you may have already had some pleasant and unpleasant passages.

Again, these canyons are not bad or evil places. Liken these descents to the inconvenience of taking your car, last serviced 50,000 miles ago, for a tune up, brake check, and fluid fill before a road trip. You hope to high heaven there is nothing seriously wrong (and that clanging noise from the engine you noticed 15,000 miles back is merely a frayed fan belt), but the potential need for some serious, up-front work definitely exists. Each canyon has been created by rivers of what might have happened and what might still happen, some self-imposed, others not. Dealing with these fickle waters can be tricky, because their eddies and rips can really wring you once or twice. No worries, though. You are built to last!

CANYON 1: BAGGAGE

Make Friends with Your Past

Have you ever looked at certain parts of your past as liabilities you simply couldn't write off, or worse, adversaries that would always win? For instance, in my own case, I walk with a limp, type with one hand, unconsciously lock and magnetically hold my right elbow to my side, slur my words when caffeinated, tired, or after a few drinks (basically all day), and can firmly shake hands only sometimes. The scar on my head can easily peek through, and the thick white lines and staple dots on my abdomen resemble the clutter of a soggy egg carton far more than a six pack. My Irish-Korean heritage rounds out my list of physical curiosities. Dealing with the trials of my parent's prolonged divorce ordeal and growing up in the jading environs of Los Angeles added additional layers of complexity and confusion to the already stressful process of "growing up."

> *"I looked up one day and saw that it was up to me.*
> *You can only be a victim if you admit defeat."*

—*The Descendents*

Ever feel like a victim? I certainly have, on more than one occasion. The sickly, comforting thing about this syndrome is that we all have the ability to look at ourselves through these cracked and myopic glasses for a multitude of "reasons": reasons of ethnic background, age, sex, sexual preference, sexual performance, parents, or growing up more than 10 minutes from the closest Blockbuster. The preceding lyrics say it all. If you admit defeat, if you knowingly turn away from your core, then yes, you are a victim, and I sincerely pity you. Something tells me you don't fit this profile, though. If you take responsibility for your past, discern a glimmer of faith in your core, and say to yourself, "You know, the only thing that can ever beat me is ME," whatever you've been through or will face, you will never, **ever** be defeated. If there is one word in the English language I absolutely despise, "victim" it is.

You may well have done things you regret—things out of spite, out of character, or out of rage or immaturity. For example, I purposefully left out my many naughty exploits when I was a studded-leather-jacket-toting punk rocker as I was trying to grapple with my past. The key here is not sweeping these events under the rug or dragging them to your mental trashcan, for no matter how hard you try, your memory has an indefatigable way of reminding you where you went wrong. Rather, you must **humbly** and **openly** face your defeats, admit your error if needed, find closure of some sort, and **then** move on. The energy derived from healing your blemishes can be invaluable, particularly as your most important asset—your LifeTime—is being devalued. You can't hope to operate at full, six-sigma capacity with these outliers still in your system.

Your past is with you wherever you go. You can't avoid it, ignore it, or relocate away from it, so why not deal with it? Per George Bernard Shaw, "If you can't get rid of the skeleton in your closet, you'd best teach it how to dance." Imagine the happiness and empowerment of being able to reflect and interact with your collective life's experiences with the candor and clarity of a good friend. The insights and feedback can be priceless and extraordinarily funny. Your high points, and even more appropriately, your low points, can serve as lucid benchmarks vis-á-vis where your journey is taking you today. Being able to draw on both as sources of strength—"Wow, look how far I've come!"—can also be incredibly exhilarating. Most importantly, your past has given you the basis for figuring out what you want your tombstone to say. The exact verbiage might still take some iterations and LifeTime, but what are good friends for other than to help you in time of need?

Make Friends with Your Future

The other potential source of your baggage is predictably your parents. (You knew they had to take a jab somewhere in this book.) For the most part, your parents are **not** bad people. They are, like you, humans with flaws, idiosyncrasies, and emotions. You know they tried their best to raise you, given their particular priorities, proficiencies, and social constructs way back when.

In this context, it is not how you were raised or where you went to school per se, but rather your parents' **expectations of you and your internalization of them** that is often the issue. A fabricated example comes from the movie *Dead Poets Society*, wherein a high school senior puts a pistol to his head after his command-and-control father shuts down his acting desires and talents, gruffly ending their final conversation with the dictum, "No, you are going to Harvard, and you will be a doctor."

As overblown as this may seem, any ideas of the number of high school kids in Japan who kill themselves when they don't score well on the national entrance exams or who don't get into the best universities? Oh yes, you say, well, they are education fanatics over there. Any idea of the percentage of American middle, high school, and college kids who partake in a variety of escapes bounding up and down the dangerous and addictive scales, sometimes unfortunately following their Asian counterparts for the same underlying reason? Children **innately** want to please their parents, a difficult fact to remember when trying to survive the daily battle. The power of these expectations can remain for LifeTimes. How many stories have you heard where the main character is "released" only on his parent's deathbed?

Often it is merely a perceived expectation (versus those clearly stated) that can linger in your memory. A friend named Lawrence recently shared a fascinating little vignette illustrating this point. He was going through his attic and happened upon an old cassette he had recorded in his youth. It was of his mother's conversation with a sitter he knew didn't like him. He had wisely set up and hidden the handheld recorder and microphone downstairs where the download would occur. At the end of the sitter's rant, you could cleanly hear the distinctive "tap tap tap" of his mother's heels on the wood floor as she marched over to the stairs and then in a strident voice demanded Lawrence come down and apologize. How kids are raised is mostly none of my business, and for all I know (and might wager), Lawrence probably deserved whatever punishment he received. It was the "tap tap" and the voice, returning after 30 years, that made Lawrence physically cringe. "You never forget the sound of your mother's voice when she is mad at you."

Being released from these invisible constraints can be simultaneously liberating and frightening. Imagine growing up with the expectation that you will one day take over your father's law practice, car dealership, bakery, or whatever. You might have a talent and passion for it; you might not. Regardless, the potential has always been there that provides a degree of future stability. Now imagine leaving all your familial connections behind and having the blessing or at least the freedom to chart your own course. It would feel like being bundled in a down coat for 20 years and then suddenly shedding it and going for a nude romp in the snow—chilled to the bone, but very alive!

This might be where you are—right now. You are cognizantly leaving a situation that is not suiting you and are looking for something better. You know it exists—I know it exists—we all know it exists. Regardless of scale or scope, change can be difficult and unnerving to instigate because you are responsible for whatever outcomes result. This, of course, is exactly what you are doing with one significant caveat: You will be **proactively** making this change happen rather than merely and passively reacting to changes around you. You will be creating an X-Factor that will improve your life and the lives of others.

So, whatever it takes—mediation, meditation, or masturbation—make sure your past and future are your friends! Intuitively, it is impossible to move happily and passionately forward if you are being constrained by your past. Don't confuse promotions, higher salary brackets, and all the other trimmings with "progress," because if you aren't happy, all the money, power, and control in the world will be wasted and are actually detrimental because they support and continue an errant focus.

People have commented, "I understand your PsychoBabble MumboJumbo, and it actually makes sense. There are some loose wires I need to connect to optimize my machine. How do I tactically start the process of making friends with my past and future?"

I ask, "Do you have a cell phone?" The answer is usually yes.

"Then get it out right now, call 411 if you need to, and start talking to whatever part of your past or future you believe might be holding you back. Life is too short not to live it on your terms."

They say talk is cheap—around five cents/minute these days—however, these sorts of conversations can be priceless. Onward to the next canyon!

CANYON 2: FINANCES

The Standard of Living Trap

Warning: The content of this section could really chafe your hide. It doesn't matter if you are making $10/hour at Wal-Mart, $100/hour as an attorney or consultant, or $1,000/hour from your portfolio. What comes next could cause intense spiritual, emotional, and worst of all, financial duress. I apologize. The truth can hurt sometimes, but it can also set you free.

The State of Your Nation

You spend too much. Don't worry—we all do. According to government data from October 2004, the national personal savings rate—the percentage of your disposable income you save—dipped to a low of 0.2%. That means you saved a whopping **$6**/month if you generated the national average income per family of $45,000. Quick question: Looking your personal budget squarely in its eye, if you were magically able to increase your income, how much on a percentage basis would you like to increase it by? Odds are, **regardless of income level**, you'd like to generate roughly a third more than you are currently grossing. Why this consistent third from blue to white collar? Maybe because that would give you just enough breathing room to be able to save more toward retirement or your kid's college, possibly pay off some debt, or tackle that needed home project—**because you are tapped out at your current level**.

A great example comes from a neighbor of mine named Bill who is an established agent of trusts and related services. His story may sound familiar. "I realized I needed to cut back. In addition to my mortgage, for a while I had two boat loans, two car loans, and a vacation house loan, all which needed monthly servicing. And I wondered why I wasn't making ends meet." He continued, "Then I noticed (consequently?) credit card statements of six and eight thousand dollars. I might bring home a nice commission check of 20 or 30 grand a particular month, but that would always seem to just get me back to where I started… I could never get ahead!"

That is the essence of the trap. As your income rises (or has risen?), so does your standard of living, and no one wants to suffer the personal or societal ignominy of scaling back your standard rather than constantly raising it; it just isn't American. More cash in gives the Brand Generalissimos the opportunity to welcome you to those "step up" products and price points that people of your (perceived) income class simply can't do without. Net sum: The more you make, the higher your monthly "fixed costs" become, severely crimping your ability to save.

Imagine suddenly receiving a salary bump of say, $30,000. What would you do? Let's say you have been driving the same car for the past eight years, and its time has come. You have always wanted a _____, which, for the past eight years has simply been out of financial reach. Now you can join a new class of driver, a rarefied echelon of sophistication and luxury for the entire world to see as you silently slip by them. You buy one with all the accoutrements: seat covers made from virgin leather personally hand-massaged by Antonio Bandera, a 64-speaker sound system, NASA satellite interfaces, the works. The thought of paying the average American mortgage payment for a maintenance visit is incidental. You are stoked. Soon, though, you realize your investment in the car and its related expenses (excise taxes, tires and brake replacement, insurance, reduced mileage, and so on) will equal one to four years of a kid's college education depending on the school, if it merely generated a 4% return for 18 years. By now, it is too late; your uniqueness had become thickly intertwined with this semiconductor on wheels (whose value declines at an astonishing clip) the moment you drove it off the lot.

At the same time, your life has been evolving. Your priorities have been shifting, resources need reallocating, and something has gotta give. You realize you may need to regress or trade down to something less sexy and less powerful—a commodity versus specialty item—and your spiritual angst is almost unbearable. No longer can you associate yourself with the sleek lines and automatically defrosting headlights of a European gem of a vehicle. You realize you are essentially suffering an identity crisis induced by your car!

How Much Is Your Identity Costing You?

This example may be a bit overblown, but it underscores a critical question: Why do you need to spend **so much** to establish or augment your identity through products as trivial and fleeting as a car (or shoes by Ferragamo, clothes by Versace, time-keeping by Rolex, and so on)? Granted, few things are as legally enjoyable as powering a high-performance vehicle through serpentine banks as professional drivers do on closed course TV ads. The issues are the costs—out of pocket and opportunity of this and other extravagances. The situation reminds me of something my mother likes to say—"It doesn't matter what you drive, it is where you can afford to live that really matters." Even after discounting her profession (real estate), her words, particularly when kids are involved, are quite wise, although they tug on another critical spring of the trap.

Personal bankruptcies (1.6 million filings occurred in 2003) are the coup de grace if the trap has snared and bled you long enough. In an excellent book by my classmate, Amelia Warren Tyagi, *The Two-Income Trap: Why Middle Class Mothers and Fathers Are Going Broke*, this problem is fully illuminated. Her research shows that there are two main drivers of this unfortunate circumstance: escalating property prices nationwide in areas where good public education still exists, and the relaxation of "usury" legislation (interesting word choice), enabling the solicitation of **five billion** offers of **$300,000** in preapproved credit card spending **per family, per year**. The net result is that families are spending a ton to live where their kids can be assured of a decent education and are floating the overruns with credit cards. Interestingly, per an article in *Boston* magazine, nearly 50% of repossessed cars in the Boston area are luxury autos. Often, the owner is so chagrined from visualizing the tow truck backing up his driveway, reverse-beeps blaring, to drag his identities away that he gives the collections agent the keys and asks him to return after dark to drive the car away.

Where you want to live is completely your decision. You may prefer to pay the exorbitant premium of living in the San Francisco area rather than enjoying yourself in upstate New York. You may prefer the year-round heat of Florida or Las Vegas, the natural beauty of Utah, the bucolic nature of the midwestern flatlands, an urban jungle, or a suburban cultural Sahara. Along with this decision comes the responsibility of ensuring you can make the necessary "reallocations" and base-level income requirements needed to keep yourself or selves out of financial harm. Running a prioritization matrix to look for potential new areas to live might be one of its best uses ever. What is important to you has a direct impact on how you should allocate your funds.

The Kid Factor (2)

In the context of family, let me offer a few words about what is potentially the most expensive adventure you may ever choose to undertake—family expansion. Kids cost money; in fact, kids can cost whatever you can make. Recent studies have pegged the cost to raise a screamin' demon through college at anywhere from a paltry $400,000 to a mere $1 million, **per demon**, with education choices and payment schemes being the largest variables. To say these expenditures do not significantly add to your standard fixed monthly costs is like unequivocally stating the earth is flat. In fact, cars aside, there is no better example of the raw power and force the trap can have than as it applies to kids…

… and for good reason. Don't you want the best you can afford of whatever—school, toys, clothing, beds, cars, neighborhoods, and so on—for your hoodlums? This said, not even kids who can climb out of a crib blindfolded can avoid the laws of cash flow. From sippee cups to strollers, furnishings to fashions, toys to treats, those marketing denizens are at it again. There is always a premium product at a premium price. Forget the Jones' new landscaping; it is the aluminum/magnesium alloy, shock-absorbed, all-wheel drive, air-conditioned, reversible, expandable, and collapsible features of the latest $400 hybrid stroller that will influence your allocations. Try to deal with this scenario like all others. Ask yourself the simple question: "What is the best I can afford?" versus "Can I afford the best?" because the latter will quite quickly entrap you.

Cash in the Bank

Per Tyagi's research mentioned earlier, the availability of "cheap" credit has made it all too easy to hide your true financial situation from yourself, particularly when those once-in-a-lifetime travel opportunities avail themselves. "Oh yeah," you reflect in passing. "This month I needed to put those surprise expenses on my credit card. No biggie. I'll pay them off next month." Unless your personal budget is gut-wrenchingly honest, these "surprise" charges will **always** magically appear, just when you least expect them. And their ability to procreate is astounding. Let me be clear: I am not suggesting axing vacations and other such expenses as long as you can accurately budget for ALL forward-looking out-flows—both fixed and variable—to ensure you can flatten these bumps as they happen. In other words, plan!

This is the ultimate takeaway of this section. The thought of working your passion, however you define it, without having **both** a tactical **and** a financial plan in place is simply unthinkable. This is what typically "delays" your plans for change for years. Knowing you can dedicate the necessary LifeTime and resources to make your metamorphosis from worker caterpillar to liberated butterfly can be difficult if you only have one month's cushion (or less) in the bank. To enable this transformation with minimal worry, you need CASH IN THE BANK, which means addressing the standard of living trap head on, no holds barred. To be clear: Defusing the trap will probably be necessary to actualize your dreams, and the more you can diffuse its power now, the more quickly you will be able to live on your terms. You cannot escape the numbers game, although remember it is a game you control and can beat. Here are a few tips on how to avoid succumbing to the standard of living trap.

Look at Your Hard Facts

You might have already faced your hardest financial fact by generating spreadsheets in the fourth P. This one routine can serve as an excellent indicator of your relative state of standard trap captivity. Hopefully you are free of its clutches, although the personal savings numbers dictate otherwise. Studies have shown that half of your frustrations and fears about your personal finances (a major driver of relationship duress) magically disappear by simply tracking and projecting your income and expenses. Including a column for actual expenses and tying things out at month's end with your bank statement is the best of all possible worlds, although this can be realistically unrealistic. The net sum here: Develop a budget, stick to it, and **always** be able to pay off all your bills the same month the charges were incurred, or start saving for projected expenses to handle those aberrant months. An insightful exercise along these lines is to write a check to your card issuer for the full amount of each purchase the day it was charged and see how much you have left at month's end. It is so easy to rob next month to pay this month. Racking up credit card debt can be a slippery and eventually expensive slope. I once shared an apartment with an accountant (of all professions) who had racked up more than one-third of his **pretax** yearly salary in credit card charges. I don't know how, or if he ever, was able to dig himself out of that hole.

Automate It. Automatically direct a certain percentage of your monthly nut to your savings accounts. Depending on your living situation, you might want to routinely include an additional slug of principal with your mortgage payment because this can dramatically reduce the time and associated interest required to retire the loan. In fact, you may want to factor this into your debt to post-tax cash flow calculations **before** committing to the mortgage.

Construct a Savings Plan. Develop milestones or goals for your savings, and incorporate these goals into your overall financial plan. I will never forget the joy I experienced when, merely two years out of college, I had been able to cobble together more than $20,000 for a property down payment with a pretax starting salary of only $18,500. Yes, this required a lot of discipline, overtime, and sacrificial offerings of short-term pleasures. The bliss of coming home and being "home" only two years out of college far surpassed any night of late-night carousing. The interesting thing is that after I had committed to this plan and budget, particularly after starting to see my savings account blossom, nothing could stop me because the goal, formerly only a dream, was now, in only a matter of months, attainable.

Invest Wisely

Plan and make your large investments in assets that can generate returns, even risky ones, rather than watching your free cash flow be devoured by usurious rent and car lease payments. Two favorite personal investments are property and education. I actually started saving for my kid's education years before I was even thinking of doing the ring thing. Aside from leveraging the power of compounding interest, it was a sure hit in the dating game! Finally, look at tax refunds as a bonus not to be spent but invested. I was able to pay for nearly a full year of business school tuition with tax refund checks.

And Finally...

Don't be a scrooge. Realize the difference between being frugal and being just plain cheap!

CANYON 3: COMMITMENT

The Corridor Principle

More often than not, it is **not** entrepreneurs' first idea that brings them fame, spotlights, and a lifetime of sandy-bottomed margaritas. Rather, it is an offshoot of their initial concept that eventually enables them to succeed, at least monetarily. The key to making this principle produce **in any context** is simply taking the first step down that terrifying, dimly lit, and dust-ridden corridor called "The Unknown," because it is **only** by making this commitment that other doors, previously unseen, will magically appear for you to open.

There is a bit of magic, or "synchronicity" as Joe Jaworski aptly calls it in a book by the same name, that surrounds you after you start down your corridor. Forces really do start to collide and collude when you publicly state your mission, whatever it may be. People know people and will make introductions on your behalf.

People will cut you deals and will go the extra step to help you. "Once you make a decision, the universe conspires to make it happen," Ralph Waldo Emerson reinforces. Why does this "network effect" mystically start? People, even random strangers, **want** you to succeed. Selfishly, everyone likes to associate himself with winners. Merely helping someone with his journey, per Laurence Rockefeller, **is** immensely satisfying.

The Corridor Principle underscores a deeper maxim:

The Hardest Part of Any Decision is Simply Making the Decision to Commit to that Decision

---

It could be figuring out what you for dinner tonight, which movie you want to see, getting married, buying a place, moving to another department in your company, looking at other work options, starting a business, or entering a new market. It doesn't matter. After you've made your full-blown commitment to the decision, believe it or not, you are already most of the way there. Ever start a business? Ever **think** of starting a business? How many months or years were you able to analyze yourself out of the decision when your gut said this was exactly what you should be doing?

The only person who can commit you to your decisions is you. If you went through the Five Ps only to say to yourself, "I am not ready for this," that's okay. If you finished the last P and thought, "Wow, I just wasted a good chunk of LifeTime on this," you have my apologies post-facto. If, having endured the journey thus far, you reflect, "Yes, I am going to make this happen!" I will personally be ecstatic. Regardless of your decision, though, please commit yourself to that decision. The last thing you should do is get into **anything** half-cocked. And if your initial decision was one of the first two cases, don't sweat it. In time, you'll be back.

THE 1 OR 0 WAKE-UP CALL

Your life has been, and will increasingly be, impacted by 1s and 0s. How is this? 1s and 0s are the essence of binary code—the fundamental building blocks of how computers work. No matter how complex or massive the problem, to computers, it all inevitably boils down to 1s and 0s. It's elegant, practical, and most of all, simple.

Fortunately, you don't operate like a computer, although using this 1 or 0 concept for specific decisions can be quite useful, particularly for those base-level choices on which you center your life. (Think matrix.) A great application of this means of selection is the 1 or 0 wake-up call. When sleep leaves you each morning, you are blessed with another day of promise and potential. It doesn't matter if you are 16 and struggling to get out of bed, 36 and roused due to something else living in your house, 56 and worried about retirement, or 76 and up just for kicks—the rising of the sun gives you one more day of opportunity to get out there, believe in your core, and have the time of your life. From my perspective, merely being able to walk, see, and communicate without assistance is an amazing present—everything else is gravy. The decision is a simple one: 1 or 0, yes or no, damn the torpedoes and full speed ahead or mope central. You either choose to give this gift called life your best shot today or you don't. And I don't believe you would ever consider yourself a 0!

ALWAYS FINISH WHAT YOU START (BEWARE OF MR. DREAMY!)

This is one of the last signposts in this canyon. Essentially, when you decide to give a particular effort your unabashed passionate "umph," see it through to wherever it might take you.

Don't look back, and don't second-guess or "what-if" the mission until you have reached your goal. Adopting this concept can measurably improve your overall performance and happiness. Imagine all the time and energy spent looking for ways to get out of commitments or extending their deadlines being refocused to the actual pursuit of the goal. Do you think projects would get done more quickly with fewer errors if this maxim was implemented?

Making this concept work requires silencing the forked tongue of a snake called Mr. Dreamy, who happens to reside in your mouth. His split palate can speak whenever you do and often seems to have a mind of his own—"My brain didn't think taking on that project was possible. In fact, my brain was dead set against it, but lo and behold, my tongue just said, 'Yes', no problem, I can do it. **What was I thinking**?" One side of his tongue makes commitments difficult to keep; the other makes commitments you simply can't keep. Should either sense a belief in its faulty expectations, Mr. Dreamy starts salivating. Unfortunately, his venom inevitably wears off, waking those bitten from their dreamlike trance to face a reality that can range in ugliness from a mere "Sorry I'm late" (and its consequences), to a lost contract, lost customer, lost promotion, or worst of all, lost confidence by those bitten. The real pisser is that this loss of confidence can often unfairly be extended from one small incident to a host of larger "areas for improvement": can't run projects successfully, lacks communication capabilities, can't forecast his or her resource needs, and so on.

How do you skin Mr. Dreamy? Here are a few ways to keep the nasty serpent at bay:

- **Trust your gut (again)**—When your brain intuitively says "No!" or even "This will be tough," let these responses drive your tongue rather than Mr. Dreamy.

This can be difficult, particularly if you are wired to wantonly please others or like the sex appeal and heroics of taking on Herculean challenges. Repeated failings, however, and the frustration, shame, costs, and so on incurred by everyone involved clearly prove that finishing what you start in a **few** cases is leagues better than partially executing many attempts. People fundamentally respect you if you can set expectations based on your abilities and then fill in the rest with the resources of others.

- **Prioritize**—The power and importance of this requirement was hopefully beaten to a pulp in the third P. No one but you and Mr. Dreamy expects you to be able to do everything. Prioritization of what is most important is critical to improving and optimizing your performance on whatever stage(s) you choose to perform. Intuitively, developing and sticking to a prioritized plan provides a significant part of the focus **and** results you need to get your train on the right track. No snake, especially Mr. Dreamy, likes to get near moving wheels.

- **Stick to your word**—This is fundamentally a 1 or 0 concept. If you say you will do something, do it—on time. It doesn't matter if it is merely "being downstairs in five minutes" or committing to delivering a software implementation in five months. Even people who have seemingly absent memories have the remarkable ability to recall the smallest unfulfilled commitments. What you say should drive your priorities and vice versa. This is downright difficult, because the serpent can influence your speech all day long. Making the effort to keep your word will quickly pay off, though, and Mr. Dreamy will skulk back to his rattan basket, tongue between his teeth. Also, don't worry if immediate traction isn't realized;

awareness is the first step of 12. Just keep at it, and when you notice improvement, give yourself a pat on the back and an extra shot of espresso in your next latte (budget permitting!).

■ **Live on your terms**—This is probably the best way to make Mr. Dreamy really lose his skin. How many times have you acquiesced to making commitments you simply don't want to, but for some silly reason, you feel obliged or compelled to? We do things for reasons of social acceptability, social status, "because I should," and so on. Whose LifeTime are you spending here? Honestly, do you think you can conjure up the requisite passion to deliver your signature excellent results if you didn't really want to do the job in the first place? Don't set yourself up to fail.

Mr. Dreamy on Paper

There is final facet to this dynamic that can directly impact your career—what you present on your résumé. Pull yours out and give it a look. If it is like the vast majority, you are either a superhuman, or you simply don't sleep just looking at everything you have excelled at. In applications to school or folks fishing for a job, the same syndrome applies. You can only hit so many targets at one time, particularly if you like to hit bulls-eyes instead of merely denting the paper encircling the circle. Not only is depth far better than breadth in understanding something, but it is also far more believable.

As an example, one cold and dreary Philadelphia afternoon, I was interviewing candidates for business school. In a rare fit of exasperation, I asked a candidate with a particularly dark and weighty Additional Pursuits section of his résumé to break down his work and pursuits by hours on a weekly basis. Excluding commuting, eating, occasional shopping for shampoo and soap, picking up dry-cleaning, getting dressed, and a robust social life, the now-sweaty candidate (who worked for a consulting firm) acknowledged that he dedicated on average 12 hours per business day solely to his work and volunteering pursuits. I then asked him how well he thought he was performing in these activities. What could he say? Through ashen smile, he recounted his successes. I had never seen a candidate want to leave an interview so quickly. Net sum: When generating your résumé or application, make it real. Mention both successes and failures, and refer to only those activities you have been able to start and finish because, like fat, padding is not transparent.

CHAPTER 12

LOOKING FOR YOUR LIFE'S WORK

Ever hear of a Greek character named Sisyphus? He offended the gods, and as penance, he had to spend eternity rolling a massive ball of stone up a rocky hill. Whenever the ball reached the summit, it would summarily roll down to the bottom, whereupon he would need to once again start pushing. No rest, coffee, or cigarette breaks. Not even a water cooler. For eternity…

To varying degrees, you might be in Sisyphus's sandals. The nature of your stone, height of your mountain, and decrees of whatever rules or rulers to whom you report are unique to you, although the metaphor can easily envelop the entire human race. Do you ever feel like no matter how hard you push, your ball of stone only gets heavier and the damn mountain never goes away? Don't you sometimes want to say, "Okay, I've done my time. You win." Do you wish you could just stop straining so bloody hard and let the stupid ball roll over your misery?

Herein sits perhaps the only set of brakes or dampers I want to introduce to your ever-accelerating success. Although it can be incredibly tempting (and daresay **legendary**) to march right up to whoever you report to (whether you like them or not) and say various versions of "See ya!" depending on your financial situation and personal burn rate, this might not be the best move, at least in the medium to long term, if it needs to happen at all. There could very well be opportunities to release your passions right under your nose at your current employer (presuming you are working there for at least one reason that fires your passion jets). Dealing with cash limitations can be an insightful and testing experience. It can also be nauseatingly frustrating, energy sapping, and excruciatingly distracting, aside from causing nontrivial dissonance with your spouse or significant other. It is definitively not for the faint of heart or those who might value their credit reports (seriously). Having kids or needing to take care of a parent adds an additional layer of accountability that you will need to confront and deal with. The last thing you want to worry about as you load, test, and reboot your next version is having the stress of making sure you can comfortably afford the license.

THE KID FACTOR (3)

The topic of hooligans again brings up an interesting caveat that deserves attention in the context of looking for your life's work. As previously observed, when kids (or other relatives, as appropriate) enter the financial picture, your priorities and the way you choose to release your passions will need to change—dramatically, in fact. Unfortunately, what often happens is that you develop a larger propensity to stick with a job you don't particularly love but one that affords you the "necessary" resources to be able to spend, nurture, and financially plan for the well-being of your offspring. As usual, there is a fine prioritization act that needs to be established and monitored to ensure that neither the providing LifeTimes nor whining LifeTimes receive inappropriate attention. This is predictably and justifiably more difficult for women due to the natural bond with their deliveries. Although it may appear to be a no-win situation, as long as your mission and releases can flex to include these fascinating fiends, the term "compromise" should not enter the realm of discussions.

Let me be clear here: If you are even vaguely contemplating taking the Pampers plunge, adapting and aligning your work and life priorities takes on an enhanced, if not paramount, importance. The last thing you want to do is raise your kids remotely, or even worse, be resentful for missing a unique and special part of life. Although there are ways to ameliorate certain requirements of your job—such as by working part time, working from home, using work-based day care, and so on—think long and hard about these options to determine if they meet your terms. If they don't for **either** partner, immediately clear the boards and get creative with other options. The studies previously mentioned consistently ranked time with loved ones as the top driver of happiness, and there is no better way to infuse your love, your core, and your passions than by imparting them in person. If you can figure this out prior to arrival (nature conveniently provides nine months to prepare), you will be at a tremendous advantage, for your personal burn rate (and LifeTime) will still be (mostly) under your control. Net sum: If you have concerns about transitioning to your life's work without kids, these issues will only magnify when you do have them.

THE POWER OF AN IMPASSIONED PLAN

You might be saying to yourself, "Where on earth will I ever find the time, energy, and space, to initiate my journey if I keep rolling my day job, with or without kids?" There is nothing more marvelous than observing the extraordinary power that comes out of nowhere from aligning and then integrating your purpose with your work. Having a plan can enable you to actualize some pretty astonishing goals, starting on the side if need be, and then, when the time is right, on a full-time basis. A significant part of this increase in productivity naturally comes from simply loving what you are doing—even those aspects you may not have liked to do in the past. For example, the turnaround in demeanor and efficiency of folks who once hated keeping tax records straight in the process of fulfilling a mission is remarkable. Passion heartily and unequivocally trumps the trivial!

By far the most refreshing part of this whole waiting game as your plan unfolds is knowing there will be an end **of your conception** and being able to systematically and tactically direct your energies to it. The details depend completely on you, your personal and financial situation, and essentially your overall openness to risk. It could be three days away, when you have arranged a meeting with your HR director to discuss alternative career paths within your company. It could be three months away, driven by how long you think you will need to find another job, or you might need to squirrel away every penny for 12 months looking at your cash flow and savings to comfortably transition or buy a business in 6. Again, this analysis really comes to life in the pro-forma section of your life summary. What is most powerful and empowering about this whole ordeal is that sooner than later, you will realize, "Wow! I really can make this happen. It doesn't matter how much additional effort this whole thing will require. **I know I am going to win!**" The frosty charge that floods your body when you encounter this point of no return is remarkably similar to feeling the icy granules of a snowball that somehow located the toasty skin between your shoulder blades.

A SISYPHEAN BALL OF SNOW

Think of your rock as representing the entirety of your life experiences—the dismal to the brilliant. Over the course of your LifeTime, it has hopefully gotten bigger and simultaneously a bit heavier. There's nothing wrong with this. You learn, grow, fail, learn, and grow again. That's life! What's critical to note is how your strength has naturally increased with its weight. In fact, the longer you have been pushing, the stronger you have become. It is this strength that will enable you to one last time force your piece of rock to the top of your mountain. This time, though, instead of flashing you its haughty "You'll-have-to-do-that-again" smile before smugly bouncing down the slope, a sudden deep freeze will envelop your peak. The decline will turn white, the smirk will start cracking, and your stone magically will become a small ball of snow, so small you can easily roll it to whatever corner of your summit and with a final hurrah, send it down a **planned** path of **your** making. You will watch your coalesced life experiences, empowered with the gravity of meaning, slowly start rolling, every turn adding another layer of confidence and resolve, eventually generating a momentum that is contagious, impervious, and potentially unstoppable! Your snowball will continue to expand. Trees will shudder as it steams by, snow banks will explode with its force, and drop-offs will do nothing but increase its energy.

How long your snowball will keep churning depends completely on you, your ability to match your mission and releases, and how adept you can become in redirecting it as might be required to accommodate your changing priorities. The descent will not occur without discomfort, either. (Have you ever hit a fir tree going 80 mph?) And there is always the possibility that a natural hot spring or particularly large crevasse will appear from nowhere and cause you to take emergency, evasive action.

This is where you are, right now. You're at the edge of your mountaintop, your snowball and all its potential at your feet. Think back to when you decided you were going to commit yourself to a goal with more than tipsy New Year's resolve. Losing weight. Getting in shape. Fixing up a room. Taking care of that dusty project list at work. Taking care of the dustier project list at home. After you start the process and have incorporated it into your daily mental and physical routines, isn't it amazing how satisfying and **easy** it is to keep that snowball rolling? Yes, the first couple of days or weeks can be unpleasant and downright brutal (particularly if your goal lacks a mission context), but after your snow starts flying, watch out!

A very good friend recently did Weight Watchers. Listening to her agony of needing to refer to the "Numbers Bible" to calculate her daily consumption was reminiscent of being forced to write daily journal entries for 11th grade English. Ten days and three lost pounds later, though, she was ecstatic. She was soon able to recite the entire volume, alphabetically **and** by point count, highest foods first. She kept at it, mealtimes returned to normal (albeit with different selections for her), and her snowball started thumping. In three months she had lost 20 pounds, and she has stayed in that range ever since.

Understanding and relating to your snowball is important for two reasons. First, although it is admirable and heroic to think you can transition your life overnight, in actuality, the process requires time and effort, and then some more. It requires time to reflect, iterate, test things, research, and think again. The first hundred yards of your descent while your ball is still relatively small and fragile naturally take the most time.

Second, the snowball accurately conveys the notion that you must make significant up-front investments to realize commensurate long-term results. The only way your snowball could appear in the first place is by repeatedly forcing your rock up your mountain. In this context, you have already expended a vast amount of the necessary and initial commitment. All you must do now is continue this commitment, albeit to a slightly different goal and set of metrics. The process will quickly become self-reinforcing, self-reliant, and most importantly, self-serving.

SAYONARA!

Your gut has won. All options at your current job or line of work simply don't work; you need out. You have reviewed your numbers and are comfortable going without income for a certain number of months. You may have been able to build a rainy day fund, have received an inheritance, are getting a severance package or some other windfall, have a couple investments you don't mind liquidating, can tap a home equity line, or can get around your monthly burn somehow. (Rent your place and road trip!) The amount and means are completely driven by your own internal openness to risk, and you are the sole controller of this function. If you are comfortable and confident with your exit strategy and its milestones, by all means, say "**SAYONARA!**" **Pull the cord, and get on with finding your life's work**! There is **no** time like the present to enjoy the present, clearly clean your mind, and focus on navigating toward your niche.

There is another way to pragmatically frame this go/no-go decision: "Is not taking the chance to live on your terms worth whatever percentage of your savings you might need to invest to achieve it?" For example, a good friend had been blessed with some lucrative investments that were worth roughly $200,000. She calculated, given her monthly burn, that she would need roughly $20,000 pre-tax (presuming she has no loss-carry forwards to offset potential gains) to comfortably last her six months to find her life's work. In straight dollar terms, she would need to invest roughly one-eighth (16.5% of her savings) not only to free herself from her blatantly unhappy and frustrated working life but to get her mind and spirit in gear to replace it with something much better. What is the greater risk here—**certain** ongoing stone pushing or the **opportunity** to live your dreams? What is this worth to you?

SHOGA NAI

The Japanese have a saying, *shoga nai*, which translated literally means "There is no other way." Implicit in this expression is the notion that all other avenues to reaching your objective have been researched, analyzed, and discounted as unworkable or downright impossible. It is usually uttered with the guttural seriousness of a Samurai warrior and the existentialism of a kamikaze pilot. No matter how taxing, tough, dangerous, or suicidal this path might seem, this is the direction you simply **must** take. There is no other way.

Your ordeal will (hopefully) not be as dire or life-threatening as it was for these icons of Japanese history. It will, though, require focus, time, iteration, and most importantly **patience**. There are no shortcuts to anywhere worth going. It is this undercurrent of patience to which you must fundamentally commit as you start edging closer to living in the time of your life.

YOU ARE READY!

References and Credits

Julie Aigner-Clark, Baby Einstein Founder.

Campbell, Joseph, *The Hero With a Thousand Faces*, Princeton: Princeton University Press. 1972.

John Cassidy, Klutz Founder.

Collins, Jim, *Good to Great*, pp. 83-87. New York: HarperCollins Publishers Inc. 2001.

Diener, Ed and Oishi, Shigehiro, "Money and Happiness: Income and Subjective Well-Being Across Nations," in E. Diener and E. M. Suh (Eds.), *Subjective Well-Being Across Cultures*, Cambridge MA: MIT Press. 2000.

Excerpts from the script based on Touchstone Pictures' copyrighted feature film *Dead Poets Society* are used by permission from Disney Enterprises, Inc.

Excerpt from *The Fellowship of the Ring* by J.R.R. Tolkien. Copyright © 1954, 1965 by J.R.R. Tolkien. Copyright © renewed 1982 by Christopher R. Tolkien, Michael H.R. Tolkien, John F.R. Tolkien, and Priscilla M.A.R. Tolkien. Reprinted by permission of Houghton Mifflin Company. All rights reserved.

Friedman, Stewart D. and Greenhaus, Jeffrey H., *Work and Family – Allies or Enemies?*, p. 36. New York: Oxford University Press, Inc. 2000.

Hadley, C. N. (2001, Fall). "Take this job and love it." *Hermes* (Columbia Business School magazine): pp. 16-19.

Jaworski, Joseph, *Synchronicity*, San Francisco: Berrett-Koehler Publishers. 1998.

Loewenstein, G. & Schkade, D. (1999). Wouldn't it be nice? Predicting future feelings. In D. Kahneman, E. Diener & N. Schwarz (Eds.), *Well-being: The Foundations of Hedonic Psychology* (pp. 85-105). New York: Russell Sage Foundation.

"Look Back and Laugh" lyrics used courtesy of Minor Threat and Dischord Records.

Moffit, Nancy, "The Two-Income Trap," *Wharton Alumni Magazine*.

Montier, James, "If It Makes You Happy", *Global Equity Strategy Report*, Dresdner Kleinwort Wasserstein. June 17, 2004.

Welch, Jack and Byrne, John A., *Jack: Straight From the Gut*. New York: Warner Books, Inc. 2001.

Will of Alfred Nobel, courtesy of The Nobel Museum, Stockholm, Sweden.

Zink CF, Pagnoni G, Martin-Skurski ME, Chappelow JC, Berns GS. "Human striatal response to monetary reward depends on saliency." *Neuron* 42:509-517, 2004.

INDEX

Index

Index

Index

Index

It's Your Move
Dealing Yourself the Best Cards in Life and Work
BY CYNDI MAXEY AND JILL BREMER

The game of life is laid out in front of you, and it's your turn to take an active role in deciding the future. In *It's Your Move: Dealing Yourself the Best Cards in Life and Work*, self-improvement specialists Cyndi Maxey and Jill Bremer explore dozens of simple techniques to maximize your effectiveness and achieve your dreams—without elaborate plans and expensive programs. From reading the rules to breaking the rules, Maxey and Bremer deliver detailed strategies based on real-life examples that are sure to give you the winning hand!

ISBN 0131424815, © 2004, 288 pp., $22.95

Having It All... And Making It Work
Six Steps for Putting Both Your Career and Your Family First
BY D. QUINN MILLS WITH
SASHA K. MATTU AND KIRSTIN HORNBY

Working 24 x 7? Putting off important life goals until it's too late? Stop! Then read *Having it All...and Making it Work*: a six-step plan for staying on track with your career—and your personal life. Drawing on his Harvard Business School seminars that deal with the problems associated with trying to pursue both career goals and personal goals, D. Quinn Mills, along with Sasha Mattu and Kirstin Hornby, introduces a realistic, actionable process that leads to balance. Learn to give up what you don't want badly enough, manage workplace culture without slipping off the fast track, involve loved ones in creating balance, and keep your life in check, no matter what happens. You can't have everything. But when it comes to what matters most, you can have it all!

ISBN 0131440225, © 2004, 144 pp., $19.95

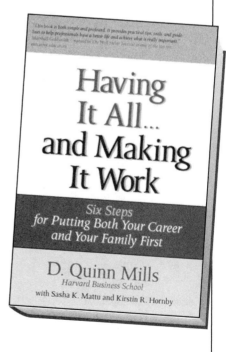